COLLECTING VINTAGE FASHION & FABRICS

PAMELA SMITH

Alliance Publishers

ISBN 0-9641509-2-1

Book and Cover Design by Cynthia Dunne
Produced by Publisher's Studio, Albany, New York

Alliance Books are available at special discounts for bulk
purchases for sales promotions, premiums, fund raising,
or educational use. For details, contact:

Alliance Publishing, Inc.
P. O. Box 080377
Brooklyn, New York 11208-0002

Distributed to the trade by
National Book Network, Inc.

10 8 6 4 2 1 3 5 7 9

Cover Credits

1. c. 1950s Kay Wilson (La Jolla, CA) grey wool cardigan with
   felt appliqués of card figures and red felt-covered buttons.
   Courtesy of Patricia Pastor, New York, NY Photo by Tom Amico.

2. c. 1920s blue and gold sequins and spangles on black silk net,
   flapper dress with side flair of black net. *Courtesy of Patricia
   Pastor, New York, NY Photo by Tom Amico.*

3. c. 1940s Palm Beach Island of Miami silk photograph tie,
   called the "Buckaroo," cowboy scene in vivid oranges and
   blues. *Courtesy of Patricia Pastor, New York, NY Photo by Tom
   Amico.*

This book is dedicated to my parents,
Gladys and John Deitrich, who gave me
an appreciation for beautiful clothing.

ACKNOWLEDGEMENTS

Many thanks to my editor and publisher, Dorothy Harris, who made this book a reality, and to Ilysa Magnus and Cindy Dunne for their assistance.

Special thanks to Harrice Simons Miller, author and friend, who taught me everything I know about collectibles!

Hugs and kisses to my children, Amy and Craig, for the enthusiasm they gave to this project. Amy's assistance and editing expertise were invaluable to me; Craig's ability to find vintage sources was extraordinary. Thank you! I love you both! Laura, we miss you.

I am very grateful to the Cedar Crest College Alumnae Museum, Cedar Crest College, Allentown, PA for sharing their museum with me and particularly to Marsha Root Walsh, Chairperson, for the time and effort she gave and her much appreciated talent in mounting dress forms.

Thank you to Susan Sargen who gave me moral support and to Dr. Arvin Murch for his patience and understanding.

Sincere thanks to Marianna Klaiman for her late night consultations, to Patricia Pastor for sharing her collection and to Tom Amico for his fine photography.

Thanks to Carrie, Moe, Hobbes and Tabetha who burned the midnight oil with me.

CONTENTS

INTRODUCTION

STYLE: PAST & PRESENT

There seems to be no limit to the number of people who find collecting vintage fashion and fabrics a way of life. More than ever before, people are realizing the treasures of the past, respecting their beauty and recycling them into their lives today. Every mother who saves a child's dress, and every bride who chooses ancestral attire, is a collector. A scrap of lace or an antique button tucked in an old sewing box can start a whole new interest. Everyone has some piece of fashion tucked away to show another generation.

In today's fads, Dad's elephant bells of the seventies turn out to be just what his son is looking for in the nineties. Those forties neckties and fifties circle skirts are just as much fun today as "yesterday." Fashion is fun and wearing vintage can be daring or different. It can remind you of another time when life was elegant or fun-loving, but most of all it is a collectible in which any of us can afford to indulge.

An important part of collecting is having enough background in your field of interest so that speaking with other collectors, shop owners or dealers will become meaningful. We have provided an insightful but easy reading guide to most aspects of collecting vintage fashion and fabrics. This is not an attempt to cover every detail. Therefore, as you develop a desire or need for more information in specific areas, there is suggested material in both *The Vintage Fashion & Fabrics Resource Guide* and bibliography.

FASHION SENSE

The fashionable wardrobe includes clothing and accessories chosen for their fine design. Vintage clothing often embody important elements of good design, such as clear lines, quality of structure, color, and texture. A vintage piece brings a unique touch to the contemporary wardrobe. The more you are exposed to vintage fashion through museums, shows, books and magazines, the easier it will be for you to recognize classic designs.

In the nineteenth century, there was a wealth of beautiful fabrics and laces that we have come to value for their quality of workmanship. The composition of these pieces is appreciated for their handwork and intricate detail. Collecting nineteenth century antique lace, trim, buttons and fine handworked pieces is another way to excite your fashion sense.

Couturiers of the twentieth century explored design concepts within the confines of the social mores of the time, and they produced many pieces that represent a timeless elegance. One example is the straight silhouette of the 1910–1920 fashion which emphasized such details as interesting drapery and unusually designed textiles of color and texture. Another is Gabrielle Chanel's relaxed style with an emphasis on simplicity. Her early clothing is as sought after today as it was in 1920.

One example of a couture style that was widely copied is the beautifully designed panne velvet jacket of the twenties and thirties. They followed a low waisted or straight line, designed for a period when elegance still reigned and fashionable women changed clothing several times a day. Today these jackets can easily be worn with a straight skirt or slim evening dress of the nineties. Finding a coat of this quality of material and design to add to your wardrobe, definitely makes fashion sense.

Bias-cut dresses, created by Madeleine Vionnet, were the rule rather than the exception in the thirties. Even today this particular style can be counted on for its classic figure-flattering lines. Sizing is the hardest part of finding a bias–cut gown; it is also difficult to find the often delicate silk fabrics in good repair. The silk or rayon day dress of the thirties with delicately patterned print is a less expensive purchase but still an uncluttered and interesting style that can be found at many vintage shops.

Ever since women joined the work force, a well-tailored jacket has been vital for a career minded wardrobe. A variety of these jackets can be found with interesting details such as large rhinestone or bakelite buttons, or a surplice front or braiding. It is even more desirable to find the jacket in black, since black is freely worn and can go anywhere, any time, any place in the nineties. When we look for timeless design in women's fashion, we immediately think of the shoulder-padded jackets of the forties, made with sequins, beading and embroidery work. A well-designed vintage jacket is well worth the price, especially when you consider this may be a unique jacket, made of a good, durable fabric, which adds distinction to your wardrobe. Remember, with all vintage clothing, beautiful design is the bonus.

Experts seem to agree that trends in vintage clothing and fabrics often parallel trends in current fashion. Designers are continually inspired by vintage pieces and incorporate them into modern dress design. If modern designers show flowing, floral chiffon, those thirties silk chiffon afternoon dresses are back in vogue. If Chinese jackets are chic this season, people will hunt out the antique ones for their originality and beautiful fabric.

Current trends are toward the softer, late forties "New Look" vintage suits for women, with classic styling and accents. Couture designer pieces, although expensive, are always valuable because of their attention to detail and quality fabric. However, classic accessories such as purses, shawls and gloves grow in popularity since they are easily added to enhance the simple, modern look. These accessories can be found in a large range of prices and styles. Fifties decorative appliquéd sweaters and forties and fifties bathing suits in mint condition are a novel addition to a wardrobe. Although hard to find, the well-made designer hats of any period are worth the effort and can be worn as a fashion statement that compliments an understated dress or suit.

Timeless style in menswear is the pure white, washable linen suit of the thirties, and two-tone shoes. Well-cut vests and vintage tuxedo jackets are classics. The battle jacket can be found in novel color combinations which add flair to conventional attire. Specialized collectors continue to add to their collections, looking for the harder-to-find items such as a Dali tie or Hollywood–designed Western shirt.

The popularity of vintage fabrics is based on the same design concept as fashion. Prints of unusual patterns or motifs (such as the simulated warp prints of the early twentieth century), bright, "printed" as opposed to "woven" cotton plaids of the thirties and forties, small prints of circus themes, people motifs, animal themes of the twenties, and the geometric deco designs of the twenties and thirties all find a place in today's design market because they are interesting and unique.

Today, vintage fashion is sold at premier auction houses and command substantial prices. Outstanding vintage clothing and textile shows have made vintage fashion a growing and popular collectible. Now more than ever before, collectors should take a discerning look at their twentieth century collections, before prices rise in five years, and we start collecting a whole new century of fashion.

OVER A CENTURY OF DESIGN & DESIGNERS

CHAPTER 1

1850–1900
COUTURE & CHANGE

Although the last half of the nineteenth century is referred to as "Victorian" for Queen Victoria, fashion was definitely Paris-inspired. In 1856, Charles Frederick Worth began his career as the first Parisian courtier, designing for the two foremost women of the time, Queen Empress Victoria of Great Britain and Empress Eugenie of France. Worth's magnificent gowns with outstanding detail and luscious fabrics were in constant demand and were imitated throughout Europe and America.

To Victorian women dress, was very important. In his introduction to the exhibition catalog, *With Grace & Favour*, Otto Charles Theime, curator of Costumes and Textiles at the Cincinnati Art Museum, stated that women of this period as well as at the turn of the century, believed that "chaste and correct appearance through dress that was tasteful, dress that was correct, and dress that was appropriate exerted a resulting positive 'moral'

5

c. late nineteenth century Russian court dress with train and bodice in royal blue velvet with floral sprays of wheat, heavily embroidered in gold. Skirt is cream silk satin, also gold embroidered. Train is over eight feet long and was worn by a member of the Imperial family or high ranking lady-in-waiting. Courtesy of Karen Augusta, North Westminster, VT.

influence on her husband, her family, and community." (p. vii) Thus, a woman's dress was seen as a reflection of her morality and of the propriety of her family and lifestyle. Fashion, therefore, was a serious endeavor and women poured over magazines like *Godey's Lady's Book, Peterson's and Harper's Bazaar*, learning the proper attire, accessories and latest Parisian styling and trim.

However, before the nineteenth century-woman could consider her outward appearance, she had to contend with the many layers of underclothes that were *de rigeur* for the fashionably dressed lady. The proper dress required undervests, drawers, a tightly laced corset, a chemise, petticoats (sometimes with cage or crinoline), an additional bustle, when fashion dictated, and stockings. On top of these underclothes were her outer garments of heavy cloth, usually a skirt and bodice. Gloves, high-laced boots, an ornamented hat and a beaded mantle completed the outfit. Patricia Cunningham, a fashion historian, estimated that such an ensemble weighed about 20 pounds.

Long skirts tended to retain dirt, corsets were too tight for breathing and exercise, and skirts were often too full to manage easily in a home or on the street. Concerns such as these motivated many dress reform movements and were initiated among feminists, health advocates, and artists who wanted to make women's clothing simpler and less threatening to their health. The two alternative styles most often advocated were bloomers, eventually used as a gym dress for calisthenics, and the classical Greek ideal of dress, simple and high-waisted, which did not see its way into fashion until about 1912.

The gowns most highly prized in the last three decades of the nineteenth century were of Parisian design. Women who could not afford to shop in Paris could order patterns or ready-mades from department stores which often required the assistance of family members or a dressmaker to complete the garment. The making of such clothing was a time-consuming occupation. Various styles came and went and women would remake many of their clothes into the new styles whenever possible. Only the very affluent were able to save dresses in their original design instead of remaking them.

The 1850 dress had a very full hoop or crinoline with a round, full skirt. Dresses in mid-century usually had a pagoda sleeve which widened at the wrist

c. 1853–1856 Evening dress of white silk taffeta with pink plush bands à disposition; trimmed with white silk bobbin lace, pink chenille, and white glass beads. Note full skirt and fashion of V-shaped trim on bodice. Courtesy of Cincinnati Art Museum. Museum Purchase: deaccession funds. Photo by Ron Forth.

over an undersleeve of lace. This style of sleeve was used in even larger proportions through the 1860s. Also during this period, dressmakers experimented with the bishop sleeve, which had a gathered shoulder and closer cuff at the wrist. The coat sleeve, a slim sleeve which curved out at the elbow using two seams, was the ensuing style, used until 1890.

Dresses were usually two pieces, skirt and bodice. In the 1850s, bodices ended at the waist and were worn with full skirts. A major fashion change of the time was the bodice which fastened in the front and flared out over the skirt, eliminating a waist seam. Later, dresses also came with slightly longer, pointed bodices over triangular-shaped skirts. Various types of pleating were used on skirts to accommodate the varieties of skirt shapes to reduce the bulk at the waist and hips. As bodices were designed to be even longer waisted, skirts were designed with gored panels in front to accommodate the bodices. These gored panel skirts drew attention to the back of the skirt; around the 1870s, this emphasis resulted in dress designs with trains.

c. early 1870s green satin dress with handmade Valenciennes lace trim on bodice and cuffs and cut steel buttons. Dress was worn by student of the college's first graduating class. Courtesy of Cedar Crest College Alumnae Museum, Allentown, PA. Photo by Tom Amico.

Left: c. 1877 wedding dress of white silk satin by Worth. Note cuirass bodice. Right: c. 1877–1878 reception dress of dark blue and pink silk satins and silk satin with warp patterning. Note fashion of panniers. Courtesy of Cincinnati Art Museum. L: Gift of Mrs. Robert Bowler through Mrs. Roger Gilman. R: Gift of Mrs. Murat Halstead Davidson. Photo by Ron Forth.

In the late 1870s, the déshabillés were first introduced. These highly decorated, loose gowns, worn in the home to receive guests, were later known as tea gowns, the one relief women had from the highly constricted fashions of the time.

In the mid-1870s, dresses had a back-swept silhouette with a large drape of fabric across the front from the waist, drawn toward the back and up to the tournure. Skirts had a great deal of pleating, shirring, and tucking. In 1880, a renewed style brought further emphasis to the hips, where fabric was used in swags, called panniers. A bodice that came down well over the hips, called the cuirass bodice, was designed in the mid-1870s and started the style for the slim silhouette that was fashionable for many years to come.

The 1890s styles included leg-of-mutton or gigot sleeved blouses worn with gored, straight-front skirts that were worn with bustles. Increasingly larger sleeves were popular until 1895, when they were modified. These styles led to the hourglass silhouette of the long-sleeved, tight-fitting blouse with high collar worn over a gently flaring, gored skirt. This look remained stylish until there was a change in corseting at the turn of the century.

c. 1890s photo of a woman wearing a leg-of-mutton blouse, gored skirt and straw boater, holding her cat.

Courtesy of the Hermitage, Ho-ho-kus, NJ.

Other Parisian courtiers, besides Charles Worth, were soon producing equally fine fashion designs. Jacques Doucet, known originally for lingerie, designed very feminine gowns. Later, Doucet's coats and outer garments helped to establish his house of couture. Madame Leferriere was known for her silks and lingerie, as well as for day dresses for Empress Eugenie. Emile Pingat was celebrated for Eastern-inspired decoration on gowns and the use of metallic embroidery. English courtier Redfern, renowned for his tailored suits, was a dressmaker for Queen Victoria.

Worth, Doucet and other couturiers also did much to improve the textile industry. Worth ordered great quantities of silks and velvets to be made in Lyons, France, a leader in silk manufacturing. The industry became known for its extravagant and beautifully made fabrics. The increased demand for these fabrics, as well as other printed cottons and silks for daily use, led to swatch services which mailed out fabric samples to subscribers, enabling them to order fabric without going to Paris. The earliest swatch service was J. Claude Frères of Paris.

Stunning photographic portrait of 1890s woman in striped silk blouse with modified leg-of-mutton sleeves, high collar and ostrich plumed straw hat with dotted net veil. Stripes were an outstanding fashion statement at this time. Courtesy of James Millinchuk, Dumont, NJ.

Page from fashion magazine, The Designer, *June, 1899. Tailor–made suit and dress. Note gored skirts with flaring at hems, tight-fitting sleeves and bodices. Straw hats were ornately trimmed.* Courtesy of the Cedar Crest College Alumnae Museum, Allentown, PA. Photo by Tom Amico.

Favorite Victorian fabrics had realistic prints of flora, feathers, wheat and grasses, leaves, vines, and soft basket weaves. Moiré silk or water silk, popular in the 1860s, got its name from its wave-like pattern of the fabric which was created by crushing the pattern into the silk as it was run through rollers.

Women wore "confections" which were shawls, cloaks and mantles. They loved the trims, ribbons and fans of point de gaze lace with ivory sticks that were imported from France. Buttons in black jet, carved ivory, porcelain, fabric and cut steel were ornaments in themselves.

Men also had a code of dress. Proper clothing had to be worn for every occasion. The frock coat in either single- or double-breasted design was the standard garment throughout the century. The sack suit was the other common choice in dress. Clothes reflected the formality of the fabrics used and the accessories that came with them. Until about 1860, embroidered vests called waistcoats were made of rich silk and brocade. Malacca walking sticks,

c. late nineteenth century opera cape of royal blue and burgundy, leaf patterned cut velvet with gold velvet and gold metallic thread embroidery. Courtesy of Alicia Trainer, Short Hills, NJ. Photo by Tom Amico.

c. 1860. Even women who could not afford a new dress ordered silk ribbons from Paris to trim bonnets and dresses. The introduction of aniline dyes in 1856 gave vivid colors to fabrics. 1. Brilliant purple roses and polka dots on white lace ribbon pattern on black silk. 2. With the advent of commerce with Japan, oriental influences were seen in fabric and trim; vivid red silk with black center line motif decorated with stitched on tufts of white threads. 3. Robin's egg blue silk with black lotus motif, edges trimmed with fine grosgrain. This kind of ribbon work is no longer done. These were done on a jacquard loom. Courtesy of Marianna Klaiman, Waldwick, NJ. Photo by Tom Amico.

gloves, and high button shoes were standard dress. Silk scarves, cravats with stickpins, stiff fabric shirts, and silk top hats were part of men's dress.

By 1880, men's clothing had a more modern appearance. The dress lounge coat, which sported silk lapels, was the forerunner to the tuxedo. The Norfolk jacket of the late nineteenth century was the country or sporting jacket, worn with knickerbockers. Bowlers, boaters, and Homburgs were the choices for hats.

c. 1880 photo of a man in bowler hat and double-breasted sack suit. Walking sticks were a popular accessory with Victorian men.

Courtesy of the Hermitage, Ho-ho-kus, NJ.

Adaptations of dress styles and fashions occurred even in the nineteenth century. Changing times required different dress. Women left their homes to go to work and everyone was encouraged to participate in athletics. However, the attention given to detail and the use of rich and beautifully made fabrics was still of primary concern and was what made nineteenth century fashions uniquely beautiful.

Important Designers and Manufacturers of the Victorian Era

Brooks Brothers: Brooks Brothers first opened in 1818 as a manufacturer of ready-to-wear men's clothing. Many of their designs were adaptations of garments worn by men in Great Britain. In 1896, they introduced the button-down collar shirt, which was copied from English rugby players. Other such adaptations of the late nineteenth and

Victorian portrait photograph of lady in a black, silk brocade bodice and silk pleated skirt with passementeries. Women often decorated clothing with elaborate roping, fringes and tassels. Note Victorian fringe parasol, fan and gloves that complete the ensemble. Courtesy of James Millinchuk, Dumont, NJ.

early twentieth centuries included the foulard tie, madras plaid, Harris tweeds from Scotland, and Shetland sweaters.

JACQUES DOUCET: In the late 1850s, Doucet was known for outerwear, referred to as "nouveautés confectionnées" by contemporaries. In the 1860s, the Doucet name is associated with women's lingerie, both custom-made and ready-to-wear. By the 1870s, women's custom-made fashions were the primary focus of the designer, with the Empress Eugenie as one important client.

DUVELLEROY: Duvelleroy designed and produced fans.

MADAME A. LEFERRIERE: Mme. Leferriere was known for her fine silks and lingerie in the Victorian era, as well as for everyday fashions.

LIBERTY & CO.: Founded by Arthur Lazenby in 1875, Liberty & Co. imported silks from the Orient, solids, and Indian or Japanese prints. They were known for their beautiful art nouveau textiles.

CHRISTOPHE-PHILIPPE OBERKAMPF: A textile mill of the nineteenth century, Oberkampf was known for its French provincial style prints with realistic, colored flowers on dark backgrounds.

EMILE PINGAT: In the 1860s, Pingat designed women's clothing, ready-to-wear and custom-made. He sold fabrics to be made into clothing, designed day dresses, ball gowns, and courtly clothing. Pingat's formal evening wear of the 1860s survives today thanks to his careful selection of silks which were hardier than those of many of his contemporary dressmakers. He trimmed his fancy gowns with laces, chenille fringe and metallic-wrapped threads. In the 1870s, Pingat designed three-piece day dresses that still show the designer's extreme devotion to detail. By 1880, Pingat was famous for his gorgeous outerwear, often worn over matching dresses.

REDFERN: One of Redfern's first designs for women was the "Jersey Lily," which was the 1879 costume worn by Lily Langtry. He also did tailored serge outfits for the active lady of this era. Since Redfern's design studio was in an English port city, his next well-known designs were 1885 women's yachting suits, traveling suits and riding habits. In 1888, Redfern was selected as dressmaker for Queen Victoria, which ensured a high profile for his Victorian designs. Redfern was heralded as a merchandising genius, with his advertisements appearing in magazines. He offered to send design sketches and samples to women unable to travel to Paris.

CHARLES FREDERICK WORTH: In 1850, Worth opened a department store in Paris, having moved from England. In France he was a favorite designer of Empress Eugenie. In the 1860s, Worth's tunic dresses, knee-length tunics over long skirts, were popular. In 1864, he made yet another change to the popular silhouette by abandoning crinolines in favor of a shorter skirt and long back train. Then, again in 1869, Worth raised the waistlines on his designs and added bustles. His designs were favorites with European royalty and international actresses. Most famous for his beautiful evening gowns, he also did more conservative traveling ensembles. He was the first designer to show his fashions on live models instead of on mannequins.

JEAN PHILLIPE WORTH: Jean Phillipe Worth was the son of Charles Worth (see above) and also designed for his father's House of Worth.

1900–1910
ELEGANT & EXTRAVAGANT

The Edwardians believed that to be well dressed one must dress appropriately. As fashion historian Elizabeth Ewing stated in her book, *History of Twentieth Century Fashion*, "Fashion was a badge of social status and its devotees regarded it with high seriousness and full absorption." (p. 10) Fashion was dictated by the aristocracy and it was considered of utmost importance to wear the correct clothing on every occasion. It was not unusual for women of leisure to change entire outfits several times a day.

The Edwardian silhouette was intricate, requiring much planning and preparation. The S-shaped corset designed by Mme. Gaches-Sarraute entirely changed the silhouette of women. It was considered a "healthier" corset because it eliminated the severe pressure on the waist and diaphragm of the previous century's corset designs. However, the new S-shaped corset was equally inhibiting, since it began low on the bust with a straight busk and extended deeply over the hips with a tightly laced back. This style corset forced the torso into a pigeon shape. Over the corset, a woman wore an impressive array of elaborate underwear, all beautifully lace-trimmed and buttoned. Taffeta and silk petticoats were added; the gowns and dresses were the final touch.

Elegant gowns and reception dresses were made of fancy fabrics: chiffon, lace, faille, silk taffeta and silk satin in cream and pastel hues. Also used at this time were the simulated warp prints, an imitation of the expensive silk warp prints of the previous century. These prints are recognizable by a blurred, out-of-focus appearance and were popular for women's apparel.

c. 1907–1908 Doucet afternoon dress of white cotton net with inset of lace and embroidered cotton. Courtesy of Cincinnati Art Museum. Gift of Miss Mary Hanna. Photo by Ron Forth.

1907 photograph of four country friends wearing typical turn-of-the-century dress with gored skirts and high-collar, embroidered cotton shirtwaists. Courtesy of Gladys Deitrich, Florham Park, NJ.

For everyday, women wore beautiful shirtwaists with tucks and lace and gored skirts. These shirt-waists and summer lingerie dresses, referred to as "whites," were made from linen, cotton, lawn or lace, with self-embroidery.

The suit in dark-colored wool or velvet was another choice of dress. The suit was widely acceptable attire, important to women who desired appropriate dress for an entire day. For women of leisure, going out in the evening or even staying at home required changes of clothing. A morning dress, a suit, a reception dress, a dinner dress, an evening dress and a tea gown were necessary

c. 1904–1906 suit with jacket, bodice and skirt of embossed navy silk velvet with embroidery and braiding. The chatelaine purse hangs from a chain and was worn clipped onto the waistband. Courtesy of Cincinnati Art Museum. Gift of Mrs. J. C. Boyd. Photo by Ron Forth.

c. 1900 burgundy red silk stripe high-collar blouse with beige lace trim and black rope and lace button accents. Courtesy of Cedar Crest College Alumnae Museum, Allentown, PA. Photo by Tom Amico.

changes in clothing depending on the time of day. The ritual of dressing was made possible only with a staff of servants to help with the preparation of attire, including laundering and sewing.

c. 1910 fringed, white kid gauntlet gloves with covered snap closure. Courtesy of Patricia Pastor, New York, NY. Photo by Tom Amico.

To balance her S-shaped silhouette, a lady would wear an immense hat, laden with plumage, flowers or fruits, and yards of ribbon. Hats were secured with ornate, often jeweled, hat pins. A fashionably dressed woman wore her hair in a pompadour which required hair to be piled high on the head, puffed out onto "rats" or pads with combs.

As with hats, kid or silk gloves were always worn. An outfit was complete only with a dainty parasol of Chantilly lace, silk or chiffon, with a carved ivory or mother-of-pearl handle. Moonstones and garnets in small drop earrings, pins, and rings were

Harper's Bazaar, *August 1904 art nouveau fashion illustration. Note flowing lines and styles of art nouveau.* Courtesy of Cedar Crest College Alumnae Museum, Allentown, PA. Photo by Tom Amico

fashionable jewelry. Fans were often painted silk, ostrich feather, or lace, with tortoise shell or mother-of-pearl sticks that were pierced or gilded. Gauze fans with sequins or spangles were also popular. Most fans were imported from Paris, London or Vienna.

The many buttons needed for these ensembles were made of Italian glass, silver, pewter, plique-a-jour, cloisonné, or covered with fabric or thread.

Edwardian handmade bobbin lace collar, light boning for support at neck, and petite covered buttons in back. Courtesy of Marianna Klaiman, Waldwick, NJ. Photo by Tom Amico.

Art nouveau floral motifs were chic for trim and fabric. Purses were small; chatelaines, reticules, hand-worked and mesh bags were common. Gowns had lace-embroidered necks and long, full sleeves with tight wrists, trains and skirts with ruching and pleating, decorated with flowers, ribbons and lace. Evening gowns were influenced by theatrical costumes. They had deep décolletage and were beautifully and intriguingly embellished. Fox fur muffs and stoles were luxurious. The most elegant finery was the tea gown, which was a loosely fitted garment with lavish trim, worn in the early evening to receive guests in the drawing room. Jacques Doucet was famous for his use of flowing fabrics, typical in tea gowns.

In 1908, there was a change in silhouette to the Empire waist, a high-waisted, one-piece dress with a long, straight skirt. For a short time, the Empire line was absorbed into the S-shape silhouette until there was a change in corseting. Styles were simpler but still elegant. In 1909, Mariano Fortuny, originally a textile designer, patented the Delphos dress, a loose, silk, finely pleated garment that hung straight from the shoulders and was weighted at the hems with glass beads.

Most women had their dresses individually made for them by dressmakers and then added finishing details themselves. Ready-mades were available but not widely used. Those not in society were hard-pressed to keep up with the fashionable and extravagant clothing of the devotees of King Edward's court. A woman of modest means spent many hours making and remodeling clothing, as well as employing the help of a dressmaker.

Edwardian men were as conscious of their fashion tastes as their female counterparts. Proper formality was very important and clothing symbolized wealth and status. As an Esquire fashion editor wrote in the book, *Esquire's Encyclopedia of Twentieth Century Men's Fashion*, (p. 110), "One must look genteel, prosperous and athletic in the broadchested fashion of Theodore Roosevelt." The suit coats were oversized, padded, long and loose. Trousers were pleated at the waistband and tapered down the legs. By mid-decade, trousers were cuffed, initially because of rain and mud. Vests were not only worn for warmth but for the pocket watch and watch fob concealed in the pockets. This decade saw a modified version of the sack suit, called a business suit, which had four buttons, very

c. 1900 brown cotton floral two-piece country skirt and blouse with embroidered bib with missing collar, pleated skirt hem and pleated sleeves. Fabrics such as this were called neats, because of their simple and small motifs. This was a popular and inexpensive fabric at the time and a basic fabric for any woman in the family.
Courtesy of Cedar Crest College Alumnae Museum, Allentown, PA.
Photo by Tom Amico.

small lapels and a shorter jacket. Winter suits were often made of serge or worsted wool and were worn with a high derby hat. In summer, suits were flannel or linen and hats were made of straw. A well-dressed gentleman always wore gloves and often carried a malacca or bamboo walking stick or cane. For formal attire, a man wore tails, a double-breasted, white waistcoat, a white bow tie with a poke collar, and high button shoes. A long overcoat and silk opera hat completed the look. Clothing designed for comfort would not become fashionable for another decade.

Important Edwardian Designers and Manufacturers

BOUÉ SOEURS: In 1900, the Boué Soeurs were known for their lingerie dresses which were all white and extremely popular because they could be easily cleaned and were practical for summer activity.

JACQUES DOUCET: Known for his opulent gowns made of lace, mousseline, satin and silk tea gowns, tailored suits, and fur-lined coats in the late nineteenth and early twentieth centuries. He used pastels and iridescent silks as well.

DUVELLEROY: Duvelleroy designed and produced fans for the Edwardian woman.

FORTUNY: Fortuny is best known for his unique pleating style, the product of a process which he patented in 1909. His pleated gowns and cloaks were dyed vivid colors with vegetable extracts. The overall effect was silk that looked like velvet. One of his most famous designs was the Delphos dress which was sleeveless or had dolman sleeves. A tubular cut dress, it was tied at the waist with a cord. His free-flowing designs were favorites of Isadora Duncan. He also had a line of designs that were adaptations of ethnic garments: the kimono, the North African burnous and djellabah, and the sari.

MADAME GEORGETTE: One of the best Parisian milliners prior to World War I, Mme. Georgette trimmed wide-brimmed straw hats with ribbon, fake flowers and veils in the Edwardian period.

GILLET: Gillet designed and manufactured shoes in the Edwardian period.

GLUYS-BROUGHELL: Gluys-Broughell designed and manufactured fans in the Edwardian period.

HELLSTERN & CO.: Known as fine designers and makers of women's shoes, Hellstern and Sons designed beaded evening slippers with heels and leather pumps with buckle decorations in the early part of the twentieth century.

LIBERTY & CO.: Liberty & Co. supplied and imported textiles with fanciful art nouveau motifs of flora and fauna.

MADAME PAQUIN: Since opening her own shop in 1891, Paquin was well-known for her romantic clothes that came to be known as "Fairyland" dresses in the teens.

PAUL POIRET: Poiret began designing on his own in 1904. He extended the corset to the hips, thereby creating a more relaxed silhouette which became the dominant style into the next decade. Poiret's 1908 designs were simple, soft gowns that differed from the tight, corseted look so popular at the time. His loose-looking designs were popular with the famous dancer Isadora Duncan, and others. In 1909, Poiret designed a collection that was heavily influenced by the Ballets Russes, with turbans, aigrettes, and harem pants in bold colors which became the fashion trend in the next decade.

REDFERN: In 1908, he helped to popularize the Grecian style with a high waist for ladies' dresses.

CAROLINE REBOUX: Renowned for her fine millinery, Caroline Reboux was a French designer of fine ladies' hats.

1910-1920
INSPIRATION & IMAGINATION

From 1910 to 1920, couture designers looked for new sources of inspiration for their fashions. The Ballets Russes of 1909 inspired couture designers to explore color and experiment with styles of dress. The foremost designer of the time, Paul Poiret, began using intense colors like red, orange, violet, blue and emerald green. He designed dramatic evening dresses with empire waists, kimono sleeves, and tunics over trouser skirts; his designs were often worn with turbans. Heavy capes of fur were worn over richly colored gowns. Madame Lanvin, equally influenced by the oriental costumes of the Ballets Russes, designed with rich materials: gold and silver lamé and brocades.

Fashion also looked to painting for inspiration. The Fauve movement introduced bright, solid

c. 1910–1912 evening dress of pink silk satin embroidered with silver metallic threads and deep pink silk chiffon brocaded with silver metallic threads; trimmed with silver metallic machine-made lace. One of the most important features of fashion in this period is the narrow skirt and use of transparent-like fabrics. Courtesy of Cincinnati Art Museum. Gift of Mrs. Christian R. Holmes. Photo by Ron Forth.

blocks of color which were incorporated into fabric patterns. Poiret was the first to employ artists such as painter Raoul Dufy to design textiles. His beautifully colored palette lent itself to the designs of unusual and unique fabrics. Artists such as Paul Iribe and George Lepape used their art in fashion illustration; some of the most beautifully executed fashion drawings are from this period.

The dominant silhouette of the decade was a straight figure. To achieve this look, a corset was cut low in the bust and had a more natural waistline. It fit closely over the hips and had an additional brassiere. These changes in underclothes left clothing designers free to experiment with many skirt styles.

Poiret is credited with the "lampshade" style—a wired, tunic top over a narrow skirt—which led to a minaret line of clothing in 1913. His most famous design was the hobble skirt of 1910, which was so narrowly tapered the wearer had difficulty maneuvering and even walking. Small slits or pleats had to be added to make walking possible. The hobble skirt was followed by the pantaloon skirt, harem pants, and the popular walking "trotteur" skirt.

Necklines gradually changed from high necks to rounded collars to V-shapes. Tambour beading and lace was often used to decorate dresses and blouses. Jackets were long and loose, trimmed with fur in the winter. Some of the most beautiful coats were designed in the teens: full length and full cut wraps, cloaks and capes, often cut from luxurious cloth and accented with beading, fur collars and cuffs.

Evening clothes remained elaborate throughout most of the decade. In 1911, one of the more unusual fashion statements was a dress with an uneven hemline and fishtail train, which was divided in two and could be worn loose or pulled between the legs to the front and made into harem pants. In 1913, couples enjoyed the new dance rage, the tango, and Lucile introduced her tango dress with a slightly flounced skirt and knee-length tunic. In 1915, sleeveless evening gowns were narrow at the hem and had décollete´ necklines and trains. Trains continued to be a fashion shown even through wartime.

There were two daytime dress styles by 1915: semi-fitted or waisted with a full skirt. By 1916, skirts were very full and bodices on dresses were very small in contrast. Waist placement varied with designer and eventually was eliminated altogether with Chanel's loose, low-waisted chemise jersey dresses, a fashion which would be the dominant theme of the next decade.

Paris fashions were copied and sold in American department stores. Unfortunately for them, Parisian designers could not receive profits from these ready-to-wear copies of their designs. With this practice, however, fashion was reaching more people and couture designs were accessible to

c. 1916 sheer cotton lawn dress with eyelet and embroidery, drop-waist and tucked at shoulders. Dress shown with lining, not original slip. Courtesy of Cedar Crest College Museum, Allentown, PA. Photo by Tom Amico.

more women. Mail order added another new dimension to fashion and ads continued to lure women with "designs from Paris."

Sports clothing gained in popularity as women participated in tennis, golf and skating. Bloomers, knickers and fur skating costumes were prevalent and gave a new freedom to women's dress that had a great impact on the fashions of the decade ahead.

During World War I, there was a scarcity of cotton and wool, so silk was used in abundance. Much of the silk was woven with metallic thread which made it heavier and more expensive; it was called weighted silk. Unfortunately, it also made the silk deteriorate more rapidly. It is hard to find pieces intact from this period. Colored dyes were in short supply so fabrics were pale. During the war, women worked in military industries and needed an alternative dress that was casual and practical. While women learned labor skills during the war effort, fashions became more versatile and less decorous, although not changing fashion entirely.

Before the war, designers such as Poiret, Paquin and Callot Soeurs reigned supreme with very fancy fashions. After the war, Chanel, Patou and Vionnet came to the foreground as the next couture designers with simpler fashions. Chemise gowns in georgette, crepe, lamé, gold and silver cloth were worn for evening. Wearing all black or all white attire was a popular fashion trend. Chanel experimented with jersey, which became her signature fabric for later clothing designs. Chanel's ensemble, called the dressmaker suit, consisted of a slim, straight skirt and cardigan, loose jacket and matching blouse. Soon, jackets were virtually shapeless with soft rounded shoulders and an optional loosely styled belt.

Early in the decade, hats were formal, decked with feathers and ribbons. These hats were thought to enhance the slimmed silhouette. As clothes took on a more relaxed feeling, hairstyles were less full and hats were closer to the head, usually of velvet

January 1918 fashion ad from Maison Maurice, Fifth Avenue, New York, featuring actress Miss Peggy Wood. Note straight silhouette and ankle–length dresses, Louis–heeled shoes and hats with low crowns but wide brims. Pictorial Review. Courtesy of Gail and Doug Heiser, Altamonte Springs, FL.

and silk, with small, unadorned brims. Evening hats were sometimes a simple large feather aigrette on a band or turban. Shoes often had high vamps and many buttons. Later, the Louis heel was the most popular shoe style. Handbags were larger because women needed to carry more belongings when they worked. Large knitted and handmade bags were especially common. Gradually, fashion trends began to reflect the emerging, independent and more active roles of women in society. Women could now choose styles reflective of their changing lifestyle.

Men's fashions were also increasingly relaxed. Suits were trimly tailored with shorter jackets, narrow sleeves and soft shoulders. Trousers were pleated and cuffed with a high waist. Evening clothes followed the same styling with noteworthy formal features like fur collared overcoats, high silk hats and well-tailored waistcoats. Bow ties were shown with resort outfits and straw Panama hats. Gloves and walking sticks still completed many an outfit as did button shoes and spats.

Important Designers and Manufacturers of the Teens

RAOUL DUFY: Dufy was an artist who worked for Paul Pioret developing dyeing techniques for fabrics in the early teens. He later became the artistic director of Bianchini-Ferier, a French fabric company for which he designed silks and brocades with strong designs and colors.

HELLSTERN & SONS: A Parisian shoe designer and maker, Hellstern & Sons was known for its leather and beaded pumps.

JEANNE LANVIN: In the teens, Lanvin's designs tended toward the romantic and feminine with her *robes de style* which remained popular through the early twenties. She also showed a line of picture dresses with decidedly Victorian shapes and embroidered ornamentation. Later in the decade, her designs reflected the influences of orientalism with her Eastern-style evening wear of velvets and satins.

LUCILE: Lucile also favored feminine styles through the teens with her tea gowns in gauze, taffeta, poplin and silk. Her name is also associated with colored underwear and pastel colors in her designs. Her hats during this decade favored more romantic styles with satin crowns and fur trim.

MADAME PAQUIN: Paquin's "Fairyland" dresses of the Edwardian era were still favorites with women in the teens. In 1913, she also showed day dresses that were designed to be worn into the evening. Aware of the increasingly active role of twentieth century women, Paquin's designs were a combination of draped and tailored lines that reflected women's need to be comfortable in their activities. Other well-known Paquin designs include her tango dresses, lingerie and fur creations.

JEAN PATOU: Jean Patou first opened a house in his own name in 1919, after a break from fashion while serving in World War I. His first collection included shepherdess dresses with Russian-style embroidery.

PAUL POIRET: In the teens, Poiret continued to bring novel changes to the current silhouette. In 1911, he introduced the hobble skirt, a design which freed the hips but confined the ankles. It was not widely adopted in common dress, although it

c. 1917–1920 orange and black silk velvet hat with soft crown, deep brim and oversize bow from Joseph G. Darlington & Co. Courtesy of Philadelphia Museum of Art. Given by the Misses Constance A. and Adelaide S. Jones.

caused a great deal of controversy. Another novel design was the "lampshade" tunic which had internal wiring to make it stand away from the body. Poiret also tried to popularize harem pants as an alternative to long skirts under tunics.

MADELEINE VIONNET: In 1912, Vionnet opened her own couture house. She closed it during World War I and continued with her innovative designs after reopening. Early in her career, Vionnet pioneered cutting on the bias and draped designs. She did not work with the corset shape but used her new cutting styles and diagonal seams to create her signature fluid lines that grew in popularity in the twenties and thirties.

THE 1920s
FRINGE & FRIVOLITY

As June Mulvagh noted in her book, *Vogue: History of Twentieth Century Fashion*, following World War I, couture was dominated by women: Chanel, designing for comfort in dress, Lanvin with feminine attire and Vionnet, known for drapery techniques which became very popular late in the decade and into the thirties. (p. 50)

In 1923, skirts were still ankle-length. The chemise style dress was straight and long, emphasizing a low waist accented by drapery or decorative trim of bows, pockets or embroidery. Caroline Reboux designed wide hats to complement the line of the long chemise, suits and coats. The chignon, a favored hairstyle early in the decade, complimented these hats.

The Exposition Internationale des Arts Décoratifs et Industriels Modernes in 1925 in Paris spawned art deco designs in fabrics. Fabrics were defined by angled lines and motifs with cut edges. Compacts, cigarette cases and a variety of mesh and envelope purses had deco design as well. The art movement in painting, Cubism, influenced fabric designs in the art deco movement and were often cited in the work of painter and fabric designer Sonia Delaunay.

Left to right: c. 1920s Vionnet "little black dress" composed of narrow V-shaped panels of black satin-backed crepe used on either side; c. 1920s Caroline Reboux appliqué cape of cream satin; c. 1920s Chanel "little beige dress" with sheer yoke, long sleeves, skirt inset with V-shaped godets meeting the hem border in a scalloped line, with narrow self-belt.
Courtesy of William Doyle Galleries, New York, NY.

General prosperity brought social change and, with Prohibition, it became fashionable to defy conventional ideas. Women won the right to vote and attitudes were changing. Fashions emphasized youth and were styled for the boyish torso. Bobbed hair, wide-open dark-rimmed eyes, lacquered nails, and made-up lips and cheeks defined the twenties woman. Clothes were simpler; heavy cotton and wool fabrics were replaced with light silks; short sleeveless dresses were fashionable. Gabrielle Chanel typified the look with her uncluttered clothing designs, including the timeless "little black dress."

The *"robe de style"* was a full-skirted, feminine, nostalgic dress of silk or taffeta with a Berthe collar and lace. Such dresses offered an alternative to the casual silhouette of the twenties and were introduced by couture designers such as Lanvin and Boué Soeurs.

The flat look brassiere emphasized the twenties silhouette and was worn with cami knickers, silk camisoles and silk teddies. Kimonos and colorful pajamas costumes were designed for comfort. There was great demand for black-seamed silk stockings and beige silk and clocked stockings with garters and garter buttons.

Shorter dresses made shoes more noticeable. Heels were curved, "Louis-heeled" pumps, sometimes decorated with rhinestones, enamel work or cloisonné. Pumps with marcasite

Fall-Winter 1924–1925, Cover of Fashion Service, *a pattern book. Gown accented with a fabric flower was very popular at the time as well as long beads and embroidered shawls.* Courtesy of Cedar Crest College Alumnae Museum, Allentown, PA. Photo by Tom Amico.

c. Early 1920s Jeanne Lanvin silk hat decorated with flowers of floral silk velvet. Hat sat low with brim at eyebrow level. Jeanne Lanvin was known for her "robes de style" in the 1920s. Courtesy of Philadelphia Museum of Art. Given by Miss Margaretta S. Hinchman.

#27 c. 1920s bone leather pumps with cutout. Note button and stitching. Courtesy of Marianna Klaiman, Waldwick, NJ; *c. 1920 black moire silk purse with rope tassel; inside powder, rouge and thin lipstick. Makeup first appeared in the 1920s.* Courtesy of Marianna Klaiman, Waldwick, NJ; *c. 1920 rose-colored silk stockings with brown foot and top.* Courtesy of Marianna Klaiman, Waldwick, NJ; *early twentieth century painted black glass buttons.* Courtesy of Marianna Klaiman, Waldwick, NJ; *carded petite painted enamel buttons.* Courtesy of Jane Kiernan, Ridgewood, NJ; *feather fan* Courtesy of Cedar Crest College Alumnae Museum, Allentown, PA; *c. 1930s surrealistic inspired metal mesh purse in crimson, pink, gold, brown, black, grey and copper swirls with blue jeweled clasp on silver frame.* Courtesy of Patricia Pastor, New York, NY. Photo by Tom Amico.

buckles, T-straps, and single-button straps were all popular for dancing.

Hats in the early twenties were turbans or brimmed hats with egret and ostrich feathers, appliqués, embroidery, beading, smocking and often faux flowers, leaves or fruit as trim. Picture hats made of straw or horsehair decked with silk flowers were still popular in the early twenties. However, the most renowned hat of this decade was the cloche, a cap hat worn low over the brow often accessorized with dangle earrings. Hat pins matched brooches with rhinestones, bits of coral, or tortoise bars. By 1929, the tricorn was another popular style.

Other accessories included embroidered shawls worn as evening wraps and buttons made from René Lalique's molded glass. Clothing was accessorized with long strands of beads or pearls, glitter bracelets and bakelite. Irene Castle, a dancer and trendsetter, established a style in the teens by wearing a bandeau across her forehead to hold her short haircut in place. This style was adopted by the young flappers of the twenties. As always, anything Parisian was popular: ribbons, laces, trims, beads, feathers, silk fabrics and silk flowers.

The emphasis on sports throughout the decade inspired a variety of clothing, from tennis to bathing suits. Suntans and dieting were fashionable as more women took to the beaches. Designers used the colors tan, black, yellow and tangerine to complement suntans. Women could now easily and affordably buy ready-made clothing in department stores. Fashion was more accessible to everyone.

In the last years of the decade, Elsa Schiaparelli introduced hand-knitted sweaters to fashion. The coat and dress ensemble was popular daywear. Dresses were colorfully printed chiffon for summer and long-sleeved satin or silk jersey with tiny prints for fall. Uneven hemlines were chic. Coats had surplice fronts and often were trimmed with

c. 1925 Herman Patrick Tappé assymetrical straw hat edged with crocheted cotton lace and grosgrain ribbon. Courtesy of Philadelphia Museum of Art. Given by Mrs. Carroll S. Tyson.

c. 1929 grey embroidery on grey silk suit with fabric covered buttons. Note length of dress and jacket and scooped neckline of the 20's. Courtesy of Cedar Crest College Alumnae Museum, Allentown, PA. Photo by Tom Amico.

Snapshot of Florence and beau- ready to go . . . He's in knickers and straw hat and she's wear- ing a typical low-waisted dress and cloche. Courtesy of Marguerite Conaty, Ho-ho-kus, NJ.

fur collars. Evening dresses were fancy, made of taffeta, mousseline, Chantilly lace or velvet, and had details like pouf skirts, décolleté backs, asymmetrical hems, and even trains. The silhouette remained long and slender throughout the twenties with an emphasis on a low waist.

Men wore suit jackets with broader shoulders and fuller sleeves, high-rise trousers and matching waistcoats. The waistcoat of the twenties was high-cut, single- or double-breasted with six buttons, with or without lapels. The cutaway and waistcoat were formal attire. On campus, the regimented striped tie was popular and the bow tie was another option. The oxford bags were a British fad of the mid-twenties, with oversized trouser legs. The Prince of Wales made the Fair Isle sweater popular. Knickers were part of a sporting man's wardrobe in various lengths and bagginess, known as plus fours, plus sixes and even plus eights. Pajamas replaced the nightshirt. Probably the most well-known men's garment of the decade was the raccoon fur coat. Walking sticks, canes of malacca with crooked handles, and mechanical canes were chic. Brown derby hats, the Homburg, and straw boaters were all worn. Shoes were worn with spats and oxfords were common.

Important Designers and Manufacturers of the 1920s

ALEXANDRINE: A French manufacturer of fine gloves, most popular between 1925 and 1930.

ARGENCE: In the twenties, Argence was most famous for their rhinestone-covered heels on pumps and boots.

BOUÉ SOEURS: Boué Soeurs favored the feminine look which had also been popular in the late teens, with the *robe de style* of taffeta and silk organdy with ribbon and lace trim.

CALLOT SOEURS: In the twenties, the Callot Soeurs added designs for day dresses to their lines of lingerie and ribbons. Their fancier dress designs were of velvet and laces with elaborate beadwork.

GABRIELLE CHANEL: In the twenties, Chanel continued to set the trends with her designs and personal wardrobe. She introduced wide-legged pants for women, known as "yachting pants," in 1920. In 1922, she showed more pants for women with her wide-cut beach pajamas. These pant styles were examples of Chanel's tendency to adapt menswear styles for women's fashions. Other examples included her belted raincoats, open-neck shirts, and blazers in beige, gray and navy. In the twenties Chanel also first showed her signature design that remains

c. 1920's emerald green silk velvet jacket, batiked with stylized vine and rose pink flowers; high, pleated collar with drawstring at nape and attached shoulder scarf. Courtesy of Deborah Larkin, Philadelphia, PA. Photo by Tom Amico.

today—jersey suits and the tweed skirt with sweater, faux pearl necklace and purse with gilt chain strap. Chanel also introduced the idea of the versatile "little black dress" in the 1920s.

LILLY DACHÉ: A milliner, Lilly Daché promoted the ubiquitous twenties cloche in several of her New York City shops. In the later twenties, she branched out and designed turbans with several different colors of velvet twisted together. This turban design became very popular in later decades.

ROSE DESCAT: Rose Descat, a French milliner, designed beautiful hats that were often copied in the United States in the twenties.

ECHO: Founded in the twenties, Echo made a name for themselves during this decade with their unique scarf designs.

JOHN V. FARWELL CO.: This Chicago-based company imported glass beaded bags from Paris. A common, inexpensive design was a reticule with a wide-striped pattern and beaded header. More expensive bags had silk headers and beaded handles. Other more expensive elements were jet or silver beads, silk linings or tortoiseshell frames. Other colors and more intricate patterns also added to the value of the bags. This particular company did not carry metal frame beaded bags in the twenties.

Ferragamo: An Italian shoe designer who moved to California in the twenties, Ferragamo was renowned for his hand-made shoes. Concerned with comfort as well as design, Ferragamo took up to thirteen measurements of toes alone. His many unique twenties designs included some Cubist and Futurist inspired shoes, geometric designs and Roman sandals with ankle laces. Ferragamo designed for Hollywood from 1923 until 1927, when he returned to Italy.

Hellstern & Sons: In the twenties, Hellstern and Sons showed three types of designs for shoes which they created in a variety of materials: bar shoes, chic boots and pumps with two- to three-inch high Louis heels. Their most frequently used materials included suede, kidskin, and dyed reptile skins. Often, they trimmed their designs with rhinestone buttons and fancy metal buckles. Boots for day and evening were a company specialty, including fetish boots with up to eleven-inch heels.

Peggy Hoyt: Hoyt was a milliner whose designs were fashionable with actresses of the twenties.

Charles James: In 1927, James opened his millinery shop in New York City, designing hats as he had in Europe under the name Charles Boucheron. His first collection of women's fashions arrived in 1928. In 1929, he showed wide-brimmed straw hats with tulle cockades.

Jantzen: An Oregon–based company, Jantzen developed the elastic or "rib" stitch in the early twenties which they used to manufacture their innovative bathing suit designs. In 1921, the company introduced the "suit that changed bathing to swimming"— an elastic one-piece bathing suit which allowed for more body movement as opposed to the bulky suits of other manufacturers. Jantzen showed sleeveless tunic styles for both men and women with scooped necks attached at the waist to trunks. They were decorated with three wide horizontal stripes. This new design caused much controversy at public beaches in the early twenties. Despite the controversy, Jantzen sold these suits widely and their signature patch of a red-suited girl in mid-dive could be seen affixed to cars and other personal belongings as well as to bathing suits.

JEANNE LANVIN: Lanvin was also known for her romantic-style dresses in the twenties, the *robe de style*. In 1921, she showed a collection with Aztec-inspired patterns and designs. Another of her famous designs was the Lanvin Breton suit of 1922 which had a short jacket decorated with small buttons and a large white collar. The suit was usually shown and worn with a sailor style hat. Lanvin also designed the ubiquitous beaded dance dress, as well as a popular wool jersey casual dress in a gold and silver checkered pattern, and dinner pajamas.

SALLY MILIGRAM: Miligram designed for her own house in the twenties and her lines also sold in major American department stores. Her popular advertisements featured famous actresses appearing in outfits named after them.

JEAN PATOU: A French designer, Patou was known in the early twenties in the United States for his sportswear. He designed golf ensembles and bathing suits as well as tennis outfits, including those worn by tennis star Suzanne Lengler, who wore calf-length pleated skirts and long cardigans. Patou's other twenties designs included Cubism-inspired sweaters, and his 1929 Princess line dresses which gave the illusion of high hips by raising the waistline. After 1924, Patou used his monogram on his designs.

CAROLINE REBOUX: A French milliner, Reboux helped to continue the popularity of the twenties cloche. In 1925, Reboux started a helmet-like version of the cloche which was very popular. It was close-fitting but ended in a square crown, often with a fedora-like dent in the middle. These new cloches were often trimmed with oversized bows and had very small, irregular brims that could be attached to the hat at the sides and front.

ELSA SCHIAPARELLI: Schiaparelli's first designs were black hand-knitted sweaters which had a white bow knit into the design, giving a *tromp l'oeil* effect. With these popular sweaters, Schiaparelli started her business and in 1928 she opened her New York City store.

VALENTINA: In the early twenties, Valentina showed designs with natural waistlines and covered bodices for order from her New York City shop. In 1926, she began designing costumes for stage productions. Valentina's clothing designs were known for their architectural lines and dramatic flair.

MADELEINE VIONNET: Vionnet's innovative cuts, which she had developed in the teens, became increasingly popular through the twenties. She used crepe de chine, gabardine, and satin for evening and afternoon dresses. Her suits had bias–cut skirts and wrap-around coats with side fasteners. Getting a smooth fit and shape were Vionnet's design goals.

WHITING AND DAVIS: Whiting and Davis was the twenties company that designed and manufactured the immensely popular mesh handbags of this decade. Their bags are almost always marked with the company trademark, either in miniature on the frame or on a tag attached to the handle or frame. Some of their most popular and widely copied designs include the 1922 "Princess Mary" purse, a silver-plated baby-fine soldered mesh bag and their "Dresden" enamel designs, mesh bags with pastel color designs in Impressionistic patterns. Whiting and Davis purses varied in price, with sterling silver and soldered bags having increased value because more workmanship was required.

THE 1930s
GLITTER & GLITZ

The dazzle of Hollywood influenced the decade of perhaps the most glamorous fashion designs of the twentieth century. Luxury, wealth and beauty were personified on the screen with actresses like platinum blonde Jean Harlow, wearing backless gowns of satin and lamé with mink stoles and diamonds. Adrian, the prominent Hollywood designer, designed classically lavish gowns with shimmering sequins on halter-topped and backless fashions. His shoulder-padded designs, popularized by Joan Crawford and Greta Garbo, came to signify the self-assured woman. Movies sold fashion and everyone wanted it.

c. 1930s Jean Patou black silk crepe evening dress, inset with black lace, outlined in silver thread in a flower and leaf pattern and embroidered with faceted, flat beads. Photo courtesy of William Doyle Galleries, New York, NY.

Even the working girl wore a tailored, double-breasted suit with a flared or pleated skirt, and a sensational hat. Suits had slightly fitted skirts with longer hemlines below waist-length jackets. Afternoon dresses were floral silk chiffons with long skirts that flaired at the knee. Required for evening were long gowns and velvet coats trimmed with fur, wraps, or lush silver fox furs, and scarves and muffs. Silk, lace-trimmed peach-colored lingerie and negligees with beading, embroidery or appliqué added to the glamour of the decade.

c. 1930s snapshot of two friends in V-neck, cap sleeve, small-print silk afternoon dresses worn with T-strap and ankle-strap shoes. Photo courtesy of Marguerite Conaty, Ho-ho-kus, NJ.

Clothing was feminine; hair was softly permed. The silhouette had a slim waist, narrow hips, and wider shoulders. Skirt lengths got longer as the day progressed: below knee in the afternoon, midcalf for tea, ankle length for dancing and full length for evening. The Depression of 1929 influenced the amount of clothing women purchased as well as what types of fabric were used. Evening gowns were made in cottons, sweaters were back for day wear and a suit was suggested as an all-day apparel that could take on many different looks.

Sportswear was widely popular. Bare midriff tops, lounging pajamas, playsuits, culottes, knee-length skiing and skating skirts, Lastex swimsuits and separates, the two-piece bathing suit and molded bathing suits with bra tops were all new ideas in the thirties.

The most important fashion accessories in the thirties were the belt and the hat. Mainbocher came out with the "glamour belt" which enabled a woman to change the look of a dress instantly. Belt buckles were art deco geometric designs in paste

c. 1930s fashionable portrait of college student Deborah Pearson Brennan, in a self-made bias cut, backless gown of silk with halter neckline and rhinestone belt buckle. Photo courtesy of Cedar Crest College Alumnae Museum, Allentown, PA.

or Bakelite with rhinestones. Rhinestone dress clips and removable collars and cuffs were also popular accessories that gave a single outfit more versatility.

Hat styles varied widely in the thirties. There were many small, knitted designs including berets of Lastex yarns, the Schiaparelli knit madcap and tams. There were also many hat styles that were humorous, like the monster-sized cartwheel hat and Schiaparelli's shoe and lambchop hat, the itsy bitsy doll hat and dunce cap style. As in other fashions, asymmetry was used for hat styles. For evening, women wore turbans and headdresses such as those designed by Chanel. The mesh chenille snood or résille caught shoulder-length hair at the nape, keeping it neat under a small hat. Veiling was often embroidered or sequined and came in four lengths: eyelash, nose, chin and belt-buckle. Tall turbans were worn tipped forward on piles of permed curls and were held in place with a band across the back of the head. Scarves were also used to hold hats in place. Hat trims could be and were anything, including fur, ribbons, flowers, feathers, jewels and fruit.

In the thirties, sandals and open-toed shoes were popular among women. Other common shoe styles were wedge heel designs and ankle strap designs. For the casual look, women wore oxfords and brogues in alligator, lizard or suede.

There was also a large variety of purses by couture designers like Paquin, who styled a sling bag, and Schiaparelli, who designed colorful suedes, shocking pink evening bag and other, more fanciful, bags. The most common shapes for purses were back strap pouches or envelope bags which came in cloth and skins. Straw handbags with fruits and vegetables were also popular, as well as top handled purses, zippered pochettes, and crescent-shaped bags. Evening purses were smaller and decorated with a variety of materials: jewels, sequins,

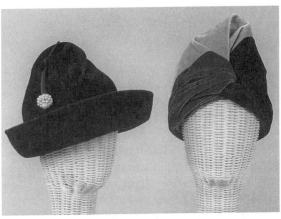

Late 1930s velour, brimmed topper hat with acrylic pearl and black stick twisted through top. Midi velour made in France "La Rose Hats, New York." Courtesy of Patricia Pastor, New York, NY; c. late 1930s tri-color velvet turban, iridescent grey/green, emerald green, and chocolate brown. "Lilly Daché, New York, Paris." Courtesy of Patricia Pastor, New York, NY. Photo by Tom Amico.

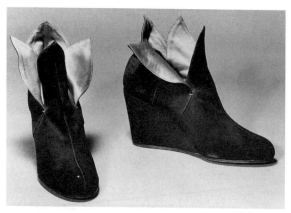

c. 1938 Salvatore Ferragamo "Ninfa" ankle boot in black suede and leather with pink silk satin lining. Courtesy of The Brooklyn Museum, 54.63.39 a&b. Gift of the Italian Government.

c. 1938 Salvatore Ferragamo "Roman Style" sandal with leather ankle strap, suede, metal framework and cork wedge. Courtesy of The Brooklyn Museum, 56.64.3 a&b. Gift of the Italian Government..

brocades, and needlepoint. Another fashionable accessory was celluloid and paper advertising fans which restaurants and shops had manufactured to hand out to their customers. Gloves were longer and were often gauntlets; they were made in a variety of colors and textures and remained a basic part of a woman's wardrobe.

Buttons tended to be somewhat whimsical, such as bakelite novelty buttons, Catalin plastic "Style-fruit", Walt Disney characters, painted buttons with native themes and plastic realistics. Buttons

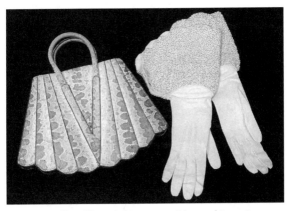

c. 1930s scalloped lizard skin purse with matching coin purse; c. 1930s ivory nubuck gloves with embroidered "Persian lamb" gauntlet. Courtesy of Patricia Pastor, New York, NY. Photo by Tom Amico.

also came in wood and glass and were sold on cards. Schiaparelli used whimsical figurine and fantasy buttons on her jackets.

Men's clothing was equally refined in the thirties. The influence on women's clothing had always been Parisian but men's styles reflected English taste. Double-breasted dinner jackets and the Windsor necktie knot were copied from the popular Duke of Windsor. The bow tie also reached its height of popularity in this decade. The narrow-shaped Indian madras bow was featured in magazines with casual wear. Hollywood-inspired neckwear, such as Humphrey Bogart's narrow, black ties was another choice. Late in the decade, polka dot ties were trendy. Wide knickers or plus fours and the popular Fair Isle sweater were worn for golfing. The collarless cardigan sweater, colorful handkerchiefs, argyle socks and the camel hair coat were typical of the time. Men wore tank top bathing suits and no top bathing suits. Trousers featured waist pleats. Half boots replaced high boots and the black patent dress shoe took hold. Lightweight felts and straws were popular hat styles from designers such as the American companies, Dobbs and Stetson, and the Italian firm, Borsolina.

Bostonian Shoe ad Esquire, *1937*. Note: *Men are wearing two-toned shoes with a double-breasted jacket and a three-piece suit and bow tie. The woman is wearing popular ankle-strap shoes.*

Esquire *fashion layout from April 1938, sporting clothes for spring; right: the plus four suit in cheviot tweed worn with a mohair knitted waistcoat and woven wool tie; left: tweed jacket with a silk foulard scarf and gray flannels.*

Palm Beach suits ad, Esquire, *July, 1937.* Courtesy of Frances Cavaricci, New York, NY.

Dobbs hat ad, Esquire, *1937, showing two styles of straw hats with large brims.* Courtesy of Frances Cavaricci, New York, NY.

Important Designers and Manufacturers of the 1930s

ADRIAN: Adrian's thirties designs commonly have bold silhouettes with dolman or kimono sleeves, long, tapered waistlines, and often diagonal fastenings. Designing for actresses such as Greta Garbo and Joan Crawford gave Adrian's hats and fashions a wide audience. Some of his most well-known designs from the thirties include the "Eugenie" hat of 1930 which was designed for Garbo and had an ostrich feather that extended over one eye; and the "Letty Lynton" dress of 1939 with wide shoulders, a narrow waist and ruffled sleeves, designed for Crawford to wear in the movie of the same name.

AGNÉS: A French milliner, Agnés's hat designs were very popular for women in the thirties.

BALENCIAGA: Balenciaga's thirties designs use somber colors and restrained lines. In 1939, he showed suits with a dropped shoulder, narrow waist and rounded hips.

A. BELLER: A manufacturer and designer of coats and suits, A. Beller used tweeds and fur in his designs. He showed tweed suits that had heavy tweed coats over lighter tweed dresses. For evening, he showed black velvet coats and jackets that had fur or metallic brocade trims. In 1931, A. Beller designed a culotte suit with front and back panels that hid the pants as a skirt; this design was called a "pantie suit."

BORSOLINA: Italian hat company renowned for their fine men's hats.

TOM BRIGANCE: In the thirties, Tom Brigance showed extensive sportswear collections featuring brightly colored linen separates: shorts, pants, skirts and bare-stomach tops.

HOUSE OF CALLOT SOEURS: In the thirties, the House of Callot Soeurs showed evening dresses of heavy satin and lamé.

HATTIE CARNEGIE: Carnegie's thirties designs were tailored suits and dresses with straight skirts. She also became known as a designer of versatile black dresses that were very popular with American women.

CATALINA: In the thirties, Catalina designed bathing suits for movie stars and promoted fan photos of the stars clad in their body-conscious designs. They also profited immensely by affiliating themselves with the Miss America pageant. These publicity ideas led to increased popularity of their mass-produced bathing suits.

GABRIELLE CHANEL: In the thirties, Chanel began to commission costume jewelry whose settings imitated those of real jewels. In the early thirties, she moved to Hollywood and designed for United Artists' films. In 1939, Chanel closed her couture house because of World War II and did not reopen it until 1954.

JO COPELAND: Designing for Patullo Modes through the thirties, Copeland's designs were fancier than her earlier sportswear designs of the twenties. She chose elegant fabrics, such as a thin wool woven with gold sequins, and was known for her use of dynamic drapery in her dress designs.

LILLY DACHÉ: This milliner opened her seven-floor shop in New York City in the late thirties. She featured profile hats, berets, turbans, and snoods as well as veiled evening hats. Daché often used intricate trimmings, with fake flowers and the occasional fake bug. In the thirties, she also had a line of hats inspired by a show of African headgear she saw in France.

DAVIDOW: A manufacturer of ready-to-wear clothing, Davidow specialized in coats and suits.

DELMAN: In the thirties, Delman was known as one of the premier shoe shops in New York. They had a contract with the famous shoe designer Vivier and featured his designs exclusively in the late thirties.

DOBBS: Men's hats.

FERRAGAMO: In the thirties, Ferragamo continued to design and produce hand-crafted shoes, such as his new wedge heels.

GOODALL CO. PALM BEACH: Fashionable men's suits and sportswear.

ELIZABETH HAWES: Hawes designed women's clothing in the thirties using natural proportions in simple designs.

HERMÈS: In the thirties, Hermès designed accessories often with coordinating sports clothes. He showed purses with watches set in them, and beach accessories (sunshades, hat, jacket and handbag.) In 1935, his "Kelly" bag was first introduced. The saddlebag-like design became increasingly popular in the fifties when it was used by Princess Grace of Monaco.

CHARLES JAMES: James's 1932 culottes design was so popular that it remained in production through the 1950s. In the mid-thirties, James designed clothing and fabrics for Paul Poiret's couture house.

JANTZEN: More revealing and clingier bathing suit styles led to innovative body-sculpting features such as the "Ladies Uplifter," which enhances the bustline with darts and elastic while offering an adjustable skirt to hide potential figure flaws. Another daring Jantzen design of the thirties was a "Wisp-O-Weight" tunic-style bathing suit which came in flesh tones, so the wearer appeared to be naked. Many of Jantzen's thirties designs used Lastex, the exciting new rubber-based fabric.

KORET (PURSES): Koret manufactured purses of reptile skins and clothes in square and rectangular shapes with short straps or handles. The handbags were often shown with coordinating shoes.

LOUISEBOULANGER: Louiseboulanger used the famous Vionnet bias cut in her elegant thirties dress designs which also had skirts that were shorter in the front than in the back.

MAINBOUCHER: Perhaps Mainboucher's most renowned thirties design was Mrs. Wallis Simpson's blue wedding dress for her marriage to the Duke of Windsor; however, his many other designs from that period included evening sweaters, dresses cut on the bias, and apron-style dresses.

CLAIRE MCCARDELL: McCardell's most innovative design of this decade came in 1938 with her so-called "monastic dress." She was inspired by a costume she had made for herself from an Algerian dress; the design was very full and flowed from the shoulders, with an optional belt. McCardell also had a line of sportswear in mostly solid colors.

EDWARD MOLYNEUX: In the thirties, Molyneux showed an orientally-inspired line of clothing designs with patterned fabrics. He also showed dirndl skirts and bias-cut dresses.

GERMAINE MONTEIL: Known as "American Vionnet, " Monteil specialized in evening dresses.

CLARE POTTER: Claire Potter designed thirties sportswear with shorts, pants, skirts and bare-stomach tops, as well as backless dresses with different jackets.

NETTIE ROSENSTEIN: Nettie Rosenstein's specialty in the thirties was evening wear of varying amounts of formality.

ELSA SCHIAPARELLI: In the thirties, Schiaparelli was known for her whimsical designs. She worked with surrealist fabrics designed by artists such as Salvador Dali and Jean Cocteau. In 1933, Schiaparelli showed a pagoda sleeve on her fashions, which also came to be known as the Egyptian look. She showed thick evening sweaters with shoulder pads, dyed fur coats and Tyrolean peasant-inspired fashions. Her 1935 collection included garments with plastic zippers featured prominently as decorative elements. In 1937, Schiaparelli designed especially humorous hats such as her shoe, lamb chop and ice cream cone hats. In 1938, Schiaparelli showed a circus collection with circus theme patterned fabrics and acrobat-shaped buttons.

c. 1930s peach silk shawl with blue, yellow, red and green floral pattern in chenille with matching fringe. Courtesy of Patricia Pastor, New York, NY Photo by Tom Amico.

SUZANNE TALBOT: Talbot's thirties designs were smaller hats that perched on the side or back of the head. Such designs were inspired by Empress Eugenie.

VALENTINA: Valentina worked in solid colors to make clean-lined garments of high-quality fabrics. Her thirties designs used many oriental design elements. Her 1937 culotte dress was inspired by the windy New York City streets in which she worked.

MADELEINE VIONNET: In the thirties, Vionnet continued to use her signature bias cut to create glamorous dresses and gowns of gabardine and crepe de chine that became immensely popular in Hollywood.

B. H. WRAGGE: B. H. Wragge designed and manufactured sportswear for women which worked with the tailored styles of menswear. Their lines of interchangeable separates in a variety of fabrics were very popular for casual dressing.

THE 1940s
ALTRUISM & ABUNDANCE

Wartime restrictions and limitations had an enormous impact on fashion. In the United States, regulations stipulated the amount and types of fabric that could be used in clothing designs. Such restrictions were also in effect in European nations. Nylon, wool and silk were in short supply, so women wore rayon crepe and black faille and, for evening clothes, velvet chiffon. Rayon gabardine was used as a replacement for wool. There were also button and pocket limitations on clothing. Standardized sizing was another result of wartime fabric rationing.

In the forties, women's clothing took on its most masculine image yet: boxy suit jackets with large shoulder pads, fitted waists, sometimes with a peplum, and narrow skirts with one or two pleats. Later, an A-line skirt was shown with suits.

Hollywood remained a serious source for fashion dictates and forties films were filled with the fashions that reflected the time: suits, sweaters, skirts, pants and bathing suits. The shoulder pad image was fashioned after Adrian's design for Joan Crawford in the 30s and made popular by Elsa Schiaparelli. Sweater sets were made famous by Hollywood's Rita Hayworth and Lana Turner.

For evening, women wore beaded sweaters and jackets. Sequins were unrationed and so were widely used on evening suits. Rhinestone buttons were a trademark of forties dresses by Eisenberg and Sons. Costume jewelry was large, mostly pins and brooches. Since there was a metal shortage, sterling silver was used by many costume jewelry manufacturers.

For other accessories, there were also wartime changes. Expensive gloves were replaced with knitted and crocheted ones. Stockings were thick rayon instead of nylon. Pocketbooks were tremendous in size and elongated. Because of the metal shortage, most handbags were made with wood or plastic closures. Designer bags by Balenciaga and Molyneux were costly but reproductions of them could easily be found in department stores. Broadcloth or calfskin were frequently used for purses and many women crocheted their own bags

c. 1940s black wool jacket with velvet beaded patches and buttons. Large buttons were typical of the decade. "Emil E. Otto, Allentown." Courtesy of Patricia Pastor, New York, NY. Photo by Tom Amico.

c. 1940 "Lucien LeLong" inside view of black cloth pleated clutch with sculptured tulip top clasp: blush, powder, perfume, lipstick, mirror and comb set in gold satin interior pockets, satin coin purse attached at center seam. Courtesy of Patricia Pastor, New York, NY. Photo by Tom Amico.

1946 bronze beaded handbag. Courtesy of Cedar Crest College Alumnae Museum, Allentown, PA. Photo by Tom Amico.

with gimp or cord. Crocheted bags were also manufactured in great numbers. Envelope bags, panier handle bags, pearlized plastic bags and hatbox bags were all designs of the forties.

In dress designs, side closures with zippers were commonly used and often there was a side drapery to the designs as well. The sweetheart neckline on dresses was very fashionable. For casual days, women wore pleated pants and print cotton dresses with patriotic motifs; polka dots and checks were also popular. Other fabric patterns were abstract designs in bold colors.

When many Parisian couture houses closed in 1940, United States manufacturers and designers had to act independently. American designers came to the forefront and were well-known in the fashion world. American designers such as Clare Potter, Claire McCardell and Carolyn Schnurer designed predominantly sportswear. Lilli Ann suits were made in San Francisco and Hattie Carnegie designed fine dresses for women in New York City.

California became known for its designer sportswear. Bathing suit manufacturers—Cole, Catalina and Mabs of Hollywood—were making names for themselves. Bathing suits had foundation styling and were made from Lastex or Celenese rayon. The two-piece suit had five inches of bare midriff, measured with exactitude.

Suits and dresses were accessorized with platform-soled shoes. Salvadore Ferragamo designed the popular cork wedge for use in place of leather and steel during the war. Suede and fabric platform sandals and mules were also fashionable. In Italy, bakelite was used for soles and heels. Ballet-style capezios were worn with casual clothes.

Forties' hats were turbans, crowned hats, calots worn at the back of the head, snoods and hand-knitted caps. The outrageous hats of the previous decade were gone in wartime. Kerchiefs tied under the chin became a chic trend and popular hairstyles were rolled or pageboys. Veils were used under the chin. Hats, gloves, veils and shoes were often ornamented with the unrestricted sequins. Homemade hats were fashioned out of whatever was available, which led to very unusual combinations. Straw was unattainable during the war so a flat, pressed felt was made out of fur and skim milk. French milliner Agnés even designed a hat from wood shavings. Toward the end of the war, hats become frivolous again and such styles as veiled turbans with fruits and flowers for decoration were designed.

Christian Dior's "New Look," shown in 1947, was a complete departure from wartime clothing. Unpadded soft rounded shoulders, wasp waists, padded hips and full skirts were suddenly all the rage. With pleating at the waist, the calf-length

c. 1948 Dior "New Look" red wool suit has soft shoul-dered jacket with peplum, black buttons on flared cuffs. "Croll and Keck." Courtesy of Patricia Pastor, New York, NY. Photo by Tom Amico.

c. 1947 Ceil Chapman black silk taffeta two–piece zippered jacket and skirt with hand-worked black beaded trim. Note skirt was pleated at waist under peplum to give fullness. Courtesy of Cedar Crest College Alumnae Museum, Allentown, PA. Photo by Tom Amico.

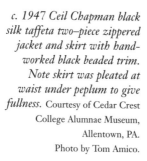

skirt could be even fuller, especially when lined with crinolines. Hats were minimal but were designed to coordinate with a specific dress. Sandals remained popular but became slimmer in the heel and toe as the Dior look became estab-lished later in the fifties. Out of the rationing and parity of wartime came affluent times and, as a result, designers showed clothing rich in fabrics and femininity.

Men's clothing also had restrictions on fabric and design. No cuffs, pleats or overlapping waistbands were made. Vests were limited and the two-piece suit became more popular than the three-piece. The backless vest was made for evening wear. Trousers were narrower and jackets shorter. Rayon, rayon blends, cheviot and flannel were used. Battle jackets were popular casual wear. The zoot suit made a brief appearance but was a waste of too much precious fabric. During its brief popularity, it was characterized by oversized coats, big shoulders, slash pockets, full knees and cuffs, trousers hiked up with suspenders and oversized bow ties.

The Hawaiian shirt, picked up by servicemen as souvenirs, became popular casual wear in the late forties. After the war, the "bold look" was how men's fashion was best described. It contrasted with the frugality and somberness of wartime clothing. Post-war fashions boasted broad shoulders, wide lapels, Borsolina brimmed hats, widespread collars, walk shorts and accessories such as large cufflinks, plaid socks and colorful ties. Indeed, colorful ties were the one mainstay of men's fashions throughout the forties. Patriotic colors had been popular early in the war and hand-painted and photo ties were popular during and after the war. These ties were vivid in color and inspired by art deco, Egyptian, African, Hawaiian and Old West motifs and colors. Ties were tied in Windsor knots and were designed by Countess Mara, Tina Leser and Jacques Fath. Arrow was a large tie manufacturer, as well as Van Heusen. After the war, Cheney manufactured pure silk ties, and luxurious clothing was again a possibility.

Important Designers and Manufacturers of the 1940s

ADRIAN: After 1942, Adrian retired from Hollywood designing and sold his designs through a Beverly Hills, California shop. His forties fashions included broad-shouldered suits with long jackets and a narrow waist, opulent ball gowns, and draped dresses for evening. He often used Pola Stout's geometric designs for fabrics as well as patterns of his own design that had animal *tromp l'oeil*, or Greek themes.

ARROW: In the 1880s, the Arrow Company was born of a merger between two firms which manufactured the widely popular, new detachable, starched collars for men's shirts. These collars continued to be the mainstay of Arrow's production through the First World War, by which time over 400 kinds of collars were marketed. Arrow switched to the production of shirts with attached collars as the demands and styles changed. After World War II, Arrow became known for popularizing the colored shirt for men. They also manufactured ties with the zany patterns of the forties.

BALENCIAGA: In the forties, he was known for his pillbox hats, and after World War II, he featured jackets with more natural-shaped waistlines and larger sleeves.

FIRA BENENSON: Known for her use of fine dressmaker details, Fira Benenson made the most of the 1943 L-85 regulations with her wide circle skirts on dresses with natural shoulders and fitted waists. Her collections of evening clothes featured décolleté necklines.

BORSOLINA: Although unavailable during the war, Borsolina hats continued to top heads of every well-dressed man in the late forties.

TOM BRIGANCE: Although he served in the war between 1942 and 1947, Tom Brigance's sportswear designs were very popular in his absence. His designs were playful, with wrap tops that bared the stomach, trousers, shorts, wrap dresses and bathing suits. He used synthetic jersey fabrics with cotton piqué and prints. His post-war designs consisted of more sportswear and sundresses, to which he also added a line of clothing suitable for city wear.

BROOKE CADWALLADER: Brooke Cadwallader was a textile designer who produced a special collection of signed scarves that had historical or current events themes. His textile designs were often used by other fashion designers. In 1947, he began designing men's silk ties and silk robes for his own label, Bronzini. All of his different designs were known for their unique color combinations; he claimed to never repeat an exact combination.

HATTIE CARNEGIE: In the forties, Hattie Carnegie had two fashion lines: an exclusive custom design business and a ready-to-wear line called Hattie Carnegie Originals. Still remembered for her fine suits and black dresses of the thirties, Carnegie also had an interest in showing different designs. During World War II, she showed a line of clothing inspired by ethnic peasant costumes. For evening, she showed dresses that resembled black sequined schoolgirl jumpers, flapper dresses with beaded fringe, and beaded and sequined suits.

CHENEY BROTHERS: Cheney Brothers were renowned for their pure silk ties. In 1947, Tina Leser designed a line of ties for this designer.

JO COPELAND: Jo Copeland designed with lines that differed from her peers designer. She showed clothes with a narrow fit, waist-length jackets, and asymmetrically decorated skirts. She used both natural and synthetic fabrics for her fashions. Her specialty was casual and formal evening dresses and suits.

COUNTESS MARA: Countess Mara designed a limited number of expensive ties, incorporating her initials into the designs.

DAVID CRYSTAL: David Crystal showed wool or cotton shirtwaist dresses and casual suits in the thirties. He also had a sportswear line of shorts, wrap skirts and tops in abstract prints in rayon.

LILLY DACHÉ: In the forties, Lilly Daché continued to design stylish hats. Her hat designs featured asymmetrical crowns and brims and side veils which tucked under the chin. Daché's wartime designs featured nap yarn hats and epaulette hats to incorporate military themes and wool restrictions. For summer, she showed hats of dressy cotton fabrics with topstitching on the brims. In 1949, she showed her first line of dresses and accessories, in addition to her hats.

DAVIDOW: Davidow manufactured wool tweed and gabardine suits in the forties.

DELMAN: As in the thirties, Delman shoes were known in the forties for their high-quality and design. A shoe manufacturer that featured young shoe designers, Delman expanded their business to include the East coast.

CHRISTIAN DIOR: Dior's 1947 "New Look" collection was perhaps the most influential fashion collection of the forties. He showed a line of shirtwaist dresses with full skirts, often lined with tulle and small waists with a hat worn on the side of the head. His 1948 collection called "Envol" showed skirts with shorter back hemlines and loose jackets with fly-away back panels and stand-away collars. In 1949, Dior showed slim skirts with back pleats and strapless evening dresses.

DOBBS: Dobbs continued to design and manufacture men's hats.

EISENBERG & SONS ORIGINALS: In 1941, Eisenberg & Sons expanded their clothing line of evening dresses to include casual clothes. They showed linen dresses for summer and wool tweed suits, coats and dresses for winter. In 1949, Eisenberg created the Eisenberg Suburban line that featured casual clothing with matching costume jewelry. Throughout the forties, Eisenberg & Sons were known for their fabulous costume jewelry pieces which were set in sterling during World War II.

JACQUES FATH: In 1949, Jacques Fath's ready-to-wear collection first appeared in the United States. He was famous for using an hourglass silhouette and his readywear line in America continued with the same curving lines. Fath was also known for popularizing stockings with Chantilly lace tops.

FERRAGAMO: In the forties, during wartime restrictions on metals, Ferragamo designed a platform heel of cork. In 1947, he designed the invisible shoe which had a clear nylon upper and bell heel.

ALIX GRÉS: Open for the first time in her own name after World War II, Alix Grés was famous for her draped designs that were often compared to classical statue garb. She used jersey, silk and wool fabrics, bias cuts and dolman sleeves to create her draped evening gowns.

I. MILLER: In the forties, I. Miller was known in New York City for high–quality shoes.

IRENE: A Los Angeles-based designer, Irene was the head costume designer for Metro-Goldwyn Meyer from 1942 to 1949. In 1947, she established a ready-to-wear line of day and evening suits with broad shoulder lines and narrow skirts. She also featured dramatic and glamorous evening dresses.

CHARLES JAMES: In 1945, Charles James established his own made-to-order collection in New York. His collections featured sculptured dresses and ball gowns that often combined different textured fabrics and odd colors in a single garment. He also showed sculptured coats and stoles of stiff fabrics as evening wraps.

JOHN-FREDERICS: In the early forties, John-Frederics hats often had attached scarves or used scarves in their designs. In the late forties, when going hatless was growing in popularity, John-Frederics featured smaller hats and campaigned heartily for the preservation of the hat.

KALMOUR: Kalmour showed inexpensive evening clothes and costume jewelry. Their evening dresses were full-skirted, made of tulle and net, and decorated with sequins and faux gems.

KNOX: Knox designed and manufactured men's hats in the forties.

KORET: Koret continued to manufacture their fine line of purses.

TINA LESER: In 1941, Tina Leser brought her resortwear collections from Honolulu to New York City and expanded her designs. She used Tahitian and Mexican fabrics, Indian sari cloth, and prints from Japanese kimonos. She favored international styles as well as the mandarin jacket and sarongs. She continued to design mostly sportswear and resortwear but also showed full skirts for evening with dolman-sleeved shrug jackets.

LILLI ANN: A San Francisco manufacturer of suits and coats of European fabrics, Lilli Ann's designs were formal enough for cocktail parties. In the late forties, Lilli Ann showed suits and coats that imitated Dior's "New Look" and others who used the earlier forties silhouette which was narrower throughout the garment.

LUCIEN LELONG: In addition to Lelong's line of clutch purses and accessories, he showed a line of clothing in 1947. His collection included slim-skirted dresses with harem hemlines and tiny-waisted suits with broad shoulders.

MAINBOUCHER: Mainboucher's forties designs were known for their versatility. Mainboucher designed with the idea that, with quick additions, his simple black dress could go from day to evening. He introduced the "glamour belt," a belt with an attached overskirt or apron that dressed up daytime outfits. He was also known for his use of everyday fabrics for evening such as dresses of eyelet and gingham. Mainboucher also designed wartime uniforms for the WAVES, Women Marines and American Red Cross.

VERA MAXWELL: In 1940, Vera Maxwell designed reefer suits for daytime with slim coats. In 1942, she used lumberjack shirt patterns with tailored suits. She also designed ethnic-inspired sportswear in 1942 showing shorts and tops with Peruvian jackets. In the late forties, Maxwell worked with the "New Look" silhouette, showing fuller skirts and pinched waists.

CLAIRE MCCARDELL: In the forties, McCardell continued to show her monk silhouette dress with an optional belt. All of McCardell's designs, from sportswear to evening, shared certain design elements: bathing suits and evening dresses with halter tops, and wrap tops with dressy pants as well as on bathing suits and on dresses. Another frequent design element on McCardell's fashions was spaghetti tie, usually meant to serve as a belt on evening and casual dresses. McCardell's sportswear was known for its practicality. She worked with large patch pockets and metal rivets as decorative elements which were also useful to the wearer. In 1942, she designed the immensely popular "popover dress" which was meant to be an all-purpose house dress. The popover dress was of topstitched denim with a wrap front, large patch pocket and attached oven mitt.

GERMAINE MONTEIL: Germaine Monteil designed expensive ready-to-wear clothing. Her favored silhouette featured a full, flared skirt which emphasized the waistline. She often showed such skirts with short jackets. For evening, Monteil designed dinner suits with long skirts and ballet-length dresses.

NORMAN NORELL: In the mid-forties, Norman Norell showed chemise dresses and tunic blouses over slim skirts with a belted waist. In 1947, he featured colored swing coats of various lengths. In the late forties, Norell experimented with different waistlines, using Empire waists and natural waists in the same dress. He also showed fur trenchcoats, pavé sequined sheath dresses for evening and wool dresses with décolleté necklines.

GOODALL CO. PALM BEACH: In the forties, the Goodall Co. continued to manufacture fashionable men's suits and sportswear.

MOLLIE PARNIS: Mollie Parnis designed inexpensive dresses with feminine styles. As the decade progressed, her skirts grew fuller and her waistlines drew more attention. She used small bows to decorate the backs of her dress designs.

PHELPS: Phelps featured handmade belts and pocketbooks with a rough-hewn look. They are commonly considered the source for the popularization of the shoulder bag.

CLARE POTTER: Clare Potter was famous for her sportswear designs, pajama costumes and loose and slim-cut pants. She would combine several contrasting colors in a single outfit. Her mid-range price designs followed a narrow, yet flowing, silhouette. She designed a forties bathing suit with bra and bloomer pants—a forerunner of the bikini.

NETTIE ROSENSTEIN: In the forties, Nettie Rosenstein designed day-to-evening black dresses, suits with patterned blouses, and dresses with matching print gloves.

ELSA SCHIAPARELLI: In the forties, Schiaparelli continued to design whimsical and humorous fashion pieces. She showed fez and turban-styled hats.

CAROLYN SCHNURER: Carolyn Schnurer designed inexpensive sportswear and bathing suits in the forties. Her casual collection included sundresses with fishnet shawls and calico bathing suits. During the war, she showed a South American-inspired line with cholo jackets. In 1947, she showed a very brief polka dot bikini.

STETSON: In the forties, Stetson designed and manufactured hats for men, as they had done for decades.

PAULINE TRIGERE: Pauline Trigere was known for her coats and dramatic but simple evening dresses. Her coat designs included officer's greatcoats and long redingotes in velvet for evening and waist-length jackets for daytime. Her evening designs used wool and taffeta in a range of styles from long to ballet-length dresses to satin evening pajamas. Her designs depended on cuts to give them shape rather than tucking and shirring. Trigere introduced the idea of removable scarves and collars on dresses and coats. She also showed dresses with jewelry attached.

VALENTINA: Valentina's daytime dress designs in the forties had a thirties look with bias cuts in silk or wool crepe. Her other designs included linen turnouts, all-season suits and evening gowns and dresses. Her evening wear ranged from floor-length, black dresses to ballet-length dance dresses and opulent ball gowns with décolleté necklines.

VAN HEUSEN: Van Heusen ties were popular in the forties. They produced three–dimensional ties in rayon and silk blend. They also manufactured men's shirts, pajamas and sport shirts.

B. H. WRAGGE: In the forties, B. H. Wragge was still designing affordable separates sportswear. His styles did not vary much beyond the annual change in color scheme and coordinating prints. Wragge's line included pleated and straight skirts, pants, jackets, dresses and blouses. In the late forties, he added turtleneck shirts, cap-sleeved and sleeveless jackets.

THE 1950s
ETIQUETTE & ELVIS

When World War II finally ended, there was a return to quiet luxury in fashion, and in life generally. People were no longer so frugal; fashions used more fabric than truly necessary; and there was a desire for a contented, conservative suburban lifestyle. Women left their wartime factory jobs and returned to homemaker roles. Families thrived in the suburbs with station wagons, picture windows, backyards, casseroles and Emily Post. The

c. 1950s Bermuda Bound-college girls off for a vaca-tion—hats, gloves, "New Look" suits, purses, and high heels. Photo courtesy of Cedar Crest College Alumnae Museum, Allentown, PA.

c. 1958 John Fredrics black lacquered wide-brimmed straw hat with silk band. Courtesy of Philadelphia Museum of Art. Gift of Elsie Focht.

focus was on the "ideal" American family. Happy role models were found on every television pro-gram. Donna Reed wore the standard daytime shirtwaist with full circle skirt, belted waist and stiff upright collar. A fancy apron was added to wear at home in the kitchen. She never left the house with-out the regulation short white gloves, flowered hat at the back of the head and suitable handbag. A more glamorous fashion ideal was typified by Audrey Hepburn's Holly Golightly of the 1961 film, "Breakfast at Tiffany's"; Holly wore a black wide-brimmed hat, simple black sheath dress, sunglasses and carried a cigarette holder.

The fashion industry boomed as Parisian and American designers provided women with new fashions every season to make up for the uniformity of the past decade. Balmain's black taffeta strapless ball gowns, Balenciaga's wide-collared evening coats, and Givenchy's extravagant cocktail dresses were lush in colors, fabrics and accessories. Evening gloves were elbow-length and even cocktail dresses had coordinating hats. Mink stoles were used as evening wraps. Women also wore cashmere sweaters with fur collars and jeweled embroidery for evening. Dior's "New Look" grew even more popular and skirts were mid-calf and pleated at the waist to give the desired fullness. Chanel returned to fashion designing, continuing

Left to right: c. 1955 Lanvin-Castillo short ball gown, in red organdy with embroidered flowers, camisole bodice and full skirt; c. 1950 Balmain ball gown in draped silk in three colors, turquoise satin for the off-the-shoulder straps, deep blue-green, ribbed silk for the torso, emerald green satin for the sweeping skirt to the floor; c. 1954 Jacques Fath short ball gown, white organdy embroidered with yellow flowers and green grass, skirt with several layers of tulle and panniers. Photo courtesy of William Doyle Galleries, New York, NY.

with her signature cardigan suit and low sling-back heel. Emilio Pucci designed silk scarves, dresses, blouses and stretch bathing suits in bold patterns of purple, blue, pink and crimson.

For casual looks, large bows accented shirtwaist dresses, gathering in the front or back. Midriffs were lightly corseted and the uplift bra gave women a new, bustier silhouette. Poodles were top dog and appeared on skirts and jewelry. The parure and costume pearls were most popular for everyday jewelry. Rhinestone-studded sunglasses were a natural part of an outfit, and toreador or capri pants and ballet slippers were worn for casual wear. Daytime sweaters were appliquéd with different motifs.

Toward the end of the decade, two entirely different silhouettes were shown. Dior designed the "sack" dress which later led to the chemise, a no-waisted dress that was short and narrow at the hem. Yves Saint Laurent produced the second innovation of the fifties in 1958—the trapeze dress. It had narrow shoulders and a triangular shape, again with no waist.

As the decade progressed, shoes became higher and heels slimmer. Dior's feminine look actually accentuated the foot. In 1955, Roger Vivier working with Dior, designed the stilleto heel, a very high, thin heel reinforced with metal, with a pointed toe. The stilleto style was used in fantastic designs for shoes and sandals with embroidery, feathers, lace, beading, rhinestones, satin and even fur. The allure of the stiletto was perpetuated by several Hollywood stars like Marilyn Monroe and

c. 1950s black straw monkey purse with brass clasp closure. Courtesy of Patricia Pastor, New York, NY. Photo by Tom Amic0.

c. 1950s kelly green felt circle skirt with three-dimensional appliqués of lobsters, seaweed, and clams with attached faux pearls. Courtesy of Patricia Pastor, New York, NY. Photo by Tom Amico.

c. 1950s striped circle cotton skirt with dolls wearing striped circle skirts. Stripes are red, yellow, blue, orange and green. Courtesy of Patricia Pastor, New York, NY. Photo by Tom Amico.

Jayne Mansfield, as well as by fashion models who stood on high heels with pelvises jutting forward, flaunting the latest fashions.

Colored eye shadow, penciled eyebrows and short haircuts were framed by many different hat styles, which reflected clothing designs in matching and contrasting colors and trim. Many women wore half hats with their suits and cocktail outfits. Bubble turbans, cloche styles, coolie chapeaux, wig hats and feather helmets were all made in a variety of fabrics including satin, velvet, jersey and fur. Short veils were shown on flowered hats and, in summer, novelty beach hats were popular.

The Wilardy lucite box-shaped handbags were popular throughout the fifties. Clutch bags were used for evening and came in a variety of fabrics, with jeweled clasps. Sets of purses and belts or purses and shoes were bestsellers. Alligator handbags with handles and lizard and snakeskin purses were also fashionable. Cavier beaded bags and decorated wooden box bags were among the sturdier bags of the decade. But the three-dimensional, straw animal and fish handbags were the best novelty designs in fifties purses.

Bathing suits were designed to sculpt the figure with elastic fibers, boned torsos, and structured bras and were given as much attention as dresses. Rose Marie Reid was the initiator of many of the highly structured styles. Cole of California mass-produced bathing suits, making the industry even larger. Hollywood screen stars now posed in swimsuits, as well as in gowns, for publicity photos.

Menswear in the fifties took a conservative turn after the "bold" look of the postwar forties. The "Mr. T" silhouette was the trim look of the decade, with narrow lapels and soft construction. Men chose gray or blue flannel suits worn with pinpoint collared shirts and narrow, small-knotted stripe or solid ties. The all-dacron suit appeared and rayon was now used year-round. Hats were *de rigeur* for men, usually with tapered crown and narrow brims.

To sport the casual look, fifties men had many choices. The Eisenhower jacket of 1950 was a waist-length, blouse-styled jacket with slant pockets and a zipper closure, made in many color variations or two-tones. Madras sport jackets, polo shirts, Bermuda shorts with native prints, colorful, tapered resort slacks, and Hawaiian shirts were all designed for the fifties. The Ivy League look was popular with button-down collared shirts in a variety of fabrics and colors.

The newest trend of the fifties was the change in fashions for youth. The American teenager was style-conscious and, for the first time fashions were designed with teens in mind. Rock 'n roll star Elvis Presley and actor James Dean became fashion idols for fifties teenagers. Rock and roll songs started fads in haircuts, suede shoes and felt skirts. Girls wore sweaters buttoned backwards and accented them with costume jewelry scatter pins. Cinch belts, bobbi socks, cuffed jeans and hair set in rollers completed the chic teenage scene. Boys wore pink shirts and khaki pants or leather jackets and greased hair. The beaches, drive-in movies and soda fountains were the new centers of teenage activity. The fifties led the way to the upcoming "youth explosion" of the sixties.

Important Designers and Manufacturers of the 1950s

ADOLFO: Adolfo's fifties millinery designs for Bergdorf Goodman spanned hat styles from miniature caps to the popular cartwheel hats.

ADRIAN: In the fifties, Adrian had a line of suits and evening clothes as well as a line of men's shirts and ties.

BALENCIAGA: In the fifties, Balenciaga showed sack dresses and varied his hemlines so that they were longer in the back than in the front. Many of his garments worked with color, block-patterned lambswool.

PIERRE BALMAIN: In 1951, Pierre Balmain's fashions were brought to the United States. A French designer, who had the reputation of bringing French style to American sizes, Balmain's collections included tailored suits, evening gowns and sheath dresses with jackets. He used stole wraps as well as Cossack-styled capes in day and evening fashions.

BILL BLASS: In the fifties, Bill Blass was the head designer for Anna Miller, who merged with the couture house of her brother Maurice Rentner in 1959. Blass got his design inspiration from thirties movies and so favored glamorous looks in his fashions. His 1959 collection featured halter necks, sequins, and long culottes.

TOM BRIGANCE: As a designer for Frank Gallant in the fifties, Tom Brigance created mostly sportswear and bathing suits. His bathing suits were strapless or halter-topped with bloomer bottoms in a variety of fabrics. These stylish suits often looked like cut-off evening dresses. In 1951, Brigance designed a corduroy pantsuit of loose pants, jacket, and top that consisted of a band of cotton fabric that went behind the neck, covering the breasts and attaching to the pants at the waistline. The effect was a bare look that left the stomach partially revealed.

PIERRE CARDIN: Through most of the fifties, Pierre Cardin had a reputation as a designer of menswear and costumes for theater productions. His first collection of men's fashions emerged in 1954; his first for women was in 1957. This new line included coats with a loose hanging back panel and bubble skirts on chemise dresses.

HATTIE CARNEGIE: In the fifties, Hattie Carnegie was known for her suits and dresses. Her bright colored wool suits had jackets that ended at the waist and straight skirts. These suits were not meant to be worn with blouses, but with necklaces. Her dresses were beaded or sequined on linen in summer, or crepes. In 1956, Hattie Carnegie died and her couture house did not continue long after her passing.

BONNIE CASHIN: In 1952, Bonnie Cashin showed "layered dressing" which meant a more casual sheath dress that could be dressed up with fancy aprons. She showed sleeveless and sleeved coats in layers as well. In the mid-fifties, Cashin designed a purse-pocket raincoat with an interior pocket designed to hold one's purse. In 1956, she featured canvas duck fabric with leather piping for pants, coats and apron skirts.

OLEG CASSINI: Cassini was known for his ultra-feminine styles in the fifties: tiny waistlines and wide skirts in taffeta and chiffon. He also showed glamorous sheath dresses, knitted suits and cocktail dresses.

GABRIELLE CHANEL: Chanel reopened her couture house in 1954, showing suit sets similar to those she showed in the thirties: coordinating tweed ensembles with pearls and gilt chain purses.

CEIL CHAPMAN: Ceil Chapman was famous for her evening dresses and gowns. Most of Chapman's designs had fitted bodices that were often strapless, with small waists and full skirts.

c. 1950s silk taffeta, orange ribbon dress with sheer overlay, feather boning in midriff and back bow. Courtesy of Cedar Crest College Alumnae Museum, Allentown, PA. Photo by Tom Amico.

Her dresses often came with coordinated stoles to complete an outfit. Chapman's 1956 and 1957 designs experimented with straighter skirts and looser bodices with V-necks.

LILLY DACHÉ: By the fifties, Lilly Daché designs could outfit a woman head-to-toe. She showed tiny hats, designed dresses and coats, and featured low-heeled fabric shoes with costume jewelry, all of her own design.

DAVIDOW: Davidow was still a well-known manufacturer of suits in the fifties. Their suits were respected for fine detailing such as repeated shapes in lapels and cutaway hems on suit jackets.

JANE DERBY: Jane Derby specialized in designs for petites. Her looks were somewhat conservative, with day and afternoon dresses in soft colored tweeds and crepes. Derby often combined traditional day and evening fabrics in an outfit.

JEAN DESSES: Jean Desses's fifties evening designs looked like Grecian robes with heavy drapery. He also showed sheath dresses with fitted jackets.

CHRISTIAN DIOR: Dior continued to be a trendsetting designer throughout the fifties. In 1950, he shortened skirts and put horseshoe collars on his dresses. Dior also used princess lines in his dress-jacket ensembles. In 1952, Dior designed a three-piece suit in pastel colors with three-quarter sleeves on a cardigan-style jacket. He also featured sheath dresses with spaghetti straps and coolie hats. In 1954, his H-line collection featured a white handkerchief, lawn jacket with soft pleats for evening. In 1955, his A- and Y-lines showed V-shaped collars and gigantic stoles, as well as long chiffon sheath dresses with spaghetti straps. Dior's 1957 collection centered around vareuse dresses. He also showed khaki bush jackets with flap pockets, and tunic dresses in black, navy blue and white.

ESTÉVEZ: In 1955, Estévez started to design for Grenelle under his name and his collections were widely popular. He specialized in black and white cocktail and evening dresses. Estevez's collection was North African-influenced, showing clothing with burnous sleeves and hoods, as well as prints that featured tiger and zebra stripes.

GALANOS: Galanos was famous for his fabulously detailed evening dresses and gowns. His designs repeatedly used chiffon to lavish excess with fifty yards to a skirt and layered cutaway collars. However, Galanos also designed narrow silhouettes with sheath and sack dresses, although he attached drapery that gave fluidity to the designs. In day wear, Galanos was one of the first designers to show horseshoe necklines on suits.

RUDI GERNREICH: In the fifties, Rudi Gernreich was known for sportswear, casual clothing and bathing suits. He used supple fabrics such as jersey in solid and geometric patterns. In 1952, he used the twenties maillot-style bathing suit without interior foundation which was in stark contrast to the highly constructed figures of other bathing suits of the day.

HUBERT GIVENCHY: Givenchy's fifties designs included bettina blouses, elegant evening dresses and gowns, and exaggerated sack-shaped, kite dresses.

GOODALL CO.: In the fifties, the Goodall Company dropped the Palm Beach company name of the thirties and forties. Regardless of the name change, Goodall continued to design fashionable suits and coats for men.

EDITH HEAD: Edith Head was a costume designer in Hollywood throughout the thirties and forties and into the fifties. One of her most widely copied designs, however, was her strapless evening dress of tulle and green satin with appliquéd white violets worn by Elizabeth Taylor in "A Place in the Sun" in 1951; Head won an Oscar for costume design for that film. Her Hollywood designs also popularized South American-styled clothing such as shirts, scarves and ponchos.

KORET: Koret manufactured fifties style purses throughout the decade.

CHARLES JAMES: Charles James's fifties designs focused on fine cuts and masterful shaping for visual interest. His evening dresses rarely had or needed any ornamentation. Department stores treated James's couture designs as they did Parisian designs, buying one couture dress design and making many quality, though less expensive, copies. James also designed suits, dresses and coats for everyday wear. He used wool fabrics, dolman sleeves and standaway collars.

JUNIOR SOPHISTICATES: In the fifties, Anne Klein was the head designer for Junior Sophisticates, creating highly fashionable designs in junior and petite sizes. She showed wool cocktail dresses and ice satin evening dresses, eschewing the typical fabric choices for her own ideas. She often used a sheath-shaped cut to which she added a bloused bodice. In 1958, Klein designed low-waisted, pleated skirted dresses as a revision of the sack dress. In the late fifties, she also showed suits and dress and jacket combinations with pea coat cuts often lined in fur.

TINA LESER: In the fifties, Tina Leser continued to look abroad for her fashion inspiration. Her 1950 collection was Spanish-inspired, with black toreador pants that ended just below the knee, ruffled white blouses, black velvet suits with red satin-lined skirts and black cloaks. Leser's sportswear designs in the fifties included sundresses shaped like Tahitian pareos, taffeta and latex bathing suits, and Lurex pajamas in ethnic-patterned fabrics.

MAINBOUCHER: In the fifties, Mainboucher designed simple yet dramatic ball gowns, versatile dresses that had optional overskirts and aprons for dressing up, and day and evening suits with boxy jackets and narrow skirts. His more casual designs for summer included coats of mattress ticking and gingham, shift dresses with appliqués and bows, and other dresses in linen and taffeta. Mainboucher also designed costumes for Broadway stage productions in the fifties.

VERA MAXWELL: Most of Vera Maxwell's designs in the fifties featured coats and jackets in ensembles, as suits or with dresses. She used warm colors and lined coats with prints to match the coordinating dresses. She used midi jacket cuts, princess line coat dresses and Chesterfield coats in her ensembles.

CLAIRE MCCARDELL: Claire McCardell's designs reflected her fashion interests in versatility and comfort. She continued to show her monastic dress designs as well as the popular popover dresses. Most of her dress designs were waistless and, included a length of spaghetti piping to serve as a belt, wherever the wearer wanted it to be. She used wool jersey, corduroy and cottons in her designs, as well as fancier fabrics in subdued colors. Many of her designs used topstitching, patch pockets and brass fasteners as functional decorations. McCardell's bathing suits were of shape-retaining fabrics and had halter necks, hoods and wrap waists. She also showed a line of short dresses and skirts for sportswear that presaged the much shorter minis of the sixties. McCardell died in 1958.

NORMAN NORELL: Norman Norell's designs in the fifties varied widely. In 1950, he showed straight chemise dresses worn with flattening bras. In 1951, he designed narrow dresses with pinched waists and short Spencer jackets. Norell's 1952 designs included suits with Norfolk jackets and hip belts as well as his famous sequined "mermaid" dresses. In 1955, he showed pea jacket suits and, in 1958, showed straight, high-waisted dresses called parachute chemises because of the straight front and bubbled back. Norell's later designs combined day and evening fashion elements such as full-skirted shirtwaist dresses in watered silks or lace and tweed jackets over satin evening gowns.

CLARE POTTER: Clare Potter designed youthful, moderately priced sportswear in the fifties. One of her most common and popular looks was a hand-knit cardigan sweater over a cotton dress or with a full, pleated skirt. She was also known for her sundresses, halter tops and bathing suits.

EMILIO PUCCI: During the fifties, Pucci designed sportswear with slim pants, capri paints, shorts and resort wear. His signature fabrics were brightly colored silks with bold patterns. His designs, especially his blouses, were popular throughout the decade and into the sixties.

ROSE MARIE REID: One of Rose Marie Reid's most well-known designs was her bathing suit with conical bosoms.

NETTIE ROSENSTEIN: In the fifties, Nettie Rosenstein used the narrow-waisted, full-skirted silhouette not only for shirtwaist dresses, but also for evening gowns and suits. She made these designs with European fabrics which had been designed specifically for her use.

YVES SAINT LAURENT: In 1958, Yves Saint Laurent designed his trapeze dress which had narrow shoulders and a short skirt. In 1959, he showed a shorter version of the hobble skirt.

SCAASI: Scaasi's specialty in the fifties was evening wear: dramatic designs with "table-top" necklines in chiffon, slipper satin and velvet. He often showed equally dramatic evening wraps that were lined to match the gowns. In 1958, Scaasi made a daring design of a knee-length evening dress with a bubble hem, being the first instance of evening fashions so short.

CAROLYN SCHNURER: Carolyn Schnurer designed mass-produced sportswear that was very affordable. She showed day dresses in French-inspired printed cottons, sleeveless sheath dresses in wool, and circle skirt ensembles with wool tube tops and matching cardigans. She quit the fashion world in the late fifties.

PAULINE TRIGERE: In the early fifties, Pauline Trigere was renowned for her seamless Princess line cuts in dresses and skirts. She rarely used shirring or tucking in her designs, but, rather, depended on darts and carefully cut panels of fabric to give her clothes shape. In the mid-fifties, Trigere showed a wool evening dress with a halter bodice that hung from a metallic neckband. In the late fifties, she designed short, strapless black dresses with a floor-length drape, as well as tunics in day suits, evening dresses, and wool day dresses.

VALENTINA: Valentina's fifties designs included suits with circle skirts and loose jackets, faille and taffeta skirts with jersey blouses, and evening gowns with optional overskirts. In the late fifties, Valentina featured her "convertible clothing" designs that allowed a travel suit to evolve into resort wear by removing a jacket and skirt to reveal shorts and a top. In 1957, Valentina closed her couture house.

WILARDY: Wilardy was a New York company which produced some of the most interesting and expensive lucite purses of the fifties.

KAY WILSON: A Los Angeles designer, Kay Wilson made wool cardigan sweaters with felt appliqué notions of particular themes.

B. H. WRAGGE: In the fifties, B. H. Wragge marketed their designs for suburban women. They showed linen sheath dresses with pongee coats and straight flannel dresses with rhinestone button fronts. Wragge's pants, shorts and sweaters were also very popular. Their practical fashions were affordably priced.

THE 1960s
FLAMBOYANT & FREE

A youth-oriented and future-minded society propelled us into the sixties. Fashion designs were streamlined. The young John F. Kennedy was elected president and Jackie Kennedy's fashionable style of dress was embraced by women across the country. John Glenn orbited the planet and designers like Pierre Cardin and André Courréges brought into the fashion sphere the space-age look, complete with helmet hats.

It was also a volatile time, and by the end of the decade we saw anti-Viet Nam War demonstrations, assassinations, riots and anti-establishment flower children on our televisions each day. Mini, maxi and midi skirts all had their heyday in fashion, as women experimented with a variety of skirt lengths. Fads came and went daily. Twiggy personified the

1967 Yves Saint Laurent beaded mini-dress of ivory organdy over pale peach silk, heavily embroidered with geometric-shaped pearlized and silver plastic pieces, surrounded by rhinestones, silver thread and crystal beads. Photo courtesy of William Doyle Galleries, New York, NY.

British mod look with her Sassoon haircut, hairpieces, lithe silhouette, mini-skirt and long legs in white lace tights. The Beatles were the "in" group of the decade and fashion looked to London for the trends of Carnaby Street.

c. 1965 James Galanos' beautifully constructed hat in wool felt. Note simplicity of line. Courtesy of Philadelphia Museum of Art. Gift of Elsie Ficht.

Oleg Cassini was Jackie Kennedy's favorite designer. He designed her high Princess–style, unbelted sleeveless dresses in solid sherbert colors, as well as suits with short jackets and large, matching fabric-covered buttons. Accessories were minimal; usually an envelope pocketbook, low heeled shoes, a pillbox hat on a slightly teased bouffant and simple "shortie" white gloves completed the ensemble.

Mary Quant was the hottest designer in Britain and the most influential. She energized the fashion industry with her mod-style clothing for the decade's "youth." Crowds of young shoppers purchased clothing in the new London boutiques, changing shopping into a new and fun experience. Flat visor hats introduced by the Beatles, shifts with cutouts and mesh midriffs, vintage clothing, boots, op-art minis and tights were fashions that could be found in boutiques. As skirts climbed higher, tights took the place of stockings and boots were made higher to meet the mini and the short-lived micro skirt. Late in the decade, Pierre Cardin showed body stockings and catsuits. Hot-colored bikinis and black mesh suits topped with flowered swim caps dominated swimsuit fashions. Lily Pulitzer customized polished cotton fabric and made it into shifts, slacks and bathing suits in tropical colors.

Shoes came in bright colors with round or square toes and low heels. Beth and Herbert Levine, influenced by the art of Andy Warhol,

c. 1960s red vinyl cloth enve-
lope purse with gold safety
pin handle, red striped cotton
lining and attached coin
purse. "Ingber, Made in
U.S.A." Courtesy of Patricia
Pastor, New York, NY. Photo
by Craig Smith.

were innovative shoe designers of the decade who used pop art styling. Plastics, imitation alligator and patent leathers were new materials for shoes. The wet look was also popular for shoes and other accessories. Boots of all lengths were especially fashionable in the sixties. Shoe designer Vivier designed footwear for Yves Saint Laurent, who showed a Mondrian-inspired line of clothing, shoes and hats. Vivier's most copied shoe was the pilgrim buckle for Laurent in 1964.

Psychedelic prints, fake fur, body painting, false eyelashes, white lipstick, hip huggers and bell bottoms were all fashion trends of the time. Outrageous fashions such as the see-through blouse and Rudi Gernreich's topless bathing suit appeared. Throwaway paper fashions were sold as inexpensive chic. Accessories included wide strap watches, lucite jewelry, fishnet stockings, chain belts, granny glasses, and hairpieces. Imitation plastic fabric was used to make funky handbags. The handmade fashions of the hippies were displayed in crocheted vests, macramé and tie dye. Fashion focused on the spirited young and their new ideas.

Men's fashions always make transitions with less fervor than women's. The sixties, however, saw a marked change in men's fashions. The double breasted suit had a new look; English styling was again very influential—wider lapels on a lightly padded jacket with side vents or a high cut, center vent. Wide, bold ties and pointed collars accessorized the fashions. Trousers went from tapered to flared with beltless waistbands and by the end of the decade appeared in a full range of fabrics and colors. Even blue jeans were made with flared legs. Jams, a Bermuda-length swimsuit in tropical print with pajama drawstring waist, were an instant success with men. For casual wear, coats varied also, as suburban men participated in many types of activities. Ski jackets, parkas, suede coats, the commuter zip-out lining coat and stadium coats were part of the wardrobe. Trench coats were shown in both midi and maxi lengths.

Men had their fashion fads as well. The leisure suit and the Nehru suit were entirely new looks in Western men's clothing. Introduced in 1966, the Nehru jacket was an exact copy of the jacket worn by Prime Minister Jawaharlal Nehru. It was copied in many fabrics for day or evening suits. The Edwardian look appeared later in the decade as a popular trend in evening wear, featuring velvet tuxedos with ruffled shirts and cuffs. The variety in men's clothing was never wider and men could choose their own individual style of dress.

Important Designers and Manufacturers in the 1960s

ADOLFO: In the sixties, Adolfo was known for the "Panama planter's hat," a mannish, brimmed straw hat, velour, and fur Cossack and pillbox hats. For evening, he designed feathered headdresses. In 1966, Adolfo began designing clothing as well as hats. His early lines were simple, such as the suede dress with low waist, gingham dirndl skirt with cotton blouse, jersey jumpsuit and organdy jumper. In the later sixties, Adolfo showed large fur berets and Renaissance and peasant looks with harem pants, vests and blouses.

LARRY ALDRICH: Larry Aldrich was known for his illusionistic, op art fabrics, as well as his more practical wool or wool jersey dinner dresses with jackets. In 1966, he showed mini dresses covered with beads. In 1969, Aldrich designed bare-stomach outfits with harem pants and full trouser styles in Quiana. In 1972, his company dissolved.

BALENCIAGA: In the sixties, Balenciago showed looser, fuller jackets with dolman sleeves and was one of the first designers to feature body stockings. Many associate his name with large buttons on suits and stand-away collars on jackets. He retired in 1968.

PIERRE BALMAIN: Balmain's designs featured empire waistlines on dresses, simple shifts, and T-line dresses with cuffs and collars.

GEOFFREY BEENE: In 1963, Geoffrey Beene first began designing independently. His clothing designs were praised as youthful and spirited. Beene showed Cossack-style dresses for evening, worn with curé's hats, as well as short skirts with long jackets, high-waisted jersey dresses and sequin-covered football sweaters for evening.

BILL BLASS: In 1963, Bill Blass's simple summer dress with ruffling at the hem and neckline was a bestseller, echoing the feminine simplicity of his earlier spaghetti-strapped evening dress of 1960. In the mid and late sixties, Blass's designs for women adopted menswear tailoring with double-breasted, wide-notched lapels, and blazers with suits and dresses. Despite the omnipresent mini skirt, Blass rarely showed any skirt that was above the knee. In 1967, he began to design for men, showing a brown velvet dinner jacket over black wool pants.

DONALD BROOKS: In 1959, Brooks began to design costumes for film, theater and television. In the early sixties, he showed plain chemise dresses and trimmed coats and stoles. In the mid-sixties, his designs grew bolder with op-art color block suits and coats, and designs with pony skin appliqués. Brooks also designed generously cut pajama styles, hooded, bias-cut wool evening dresses embroidered with sequins or bugle beads, and hippie-inspired turnouts.

PIERRE CARDIN: Cardin's sixteen designs were bright and somewhat wild. He showed colored wigs, cut-out dresses, body stockings, bias–cut spiral dresses and flared coats with large patch pockets. In 1962, he opened a boutique in Bonwit Teller featuring his men's designs. Cardin's 1964 collection was called "Space-Age" and featured knit cat suits, tight leather pants, helmets and jumpsuits. In the late sixties, Cardin brought necklines to new depths both in front and in back in women's fashions and then shortened his skirts another four inches.

OLEG CASSINI: In 1961, Oleg Cassini became the official designer for Jacqueline Kennedy. His styles were simple and somewhat fitted. Two of his most widely copied designs were the sleeveless, high-waisted evening dress with a single fabric rose for decoration and a boxy jacketed suit with fabric-covered buttons. He also had a ready-to-wear line which carried evening and cocktail dresses along the same line as the designs he did for the First Lady. In 1963, Cassini included bathing suits, sportswear, underclothes and accessories in his fashion lines. He also designed for men in the sixties.

GABRIELLE CHANEL: In the sixties, Chanel continued to show her signature suit ensembles.

OSSIE CLARK: Ossie Clark is known for her revealing designs of satin jersey and chiffon with deep necklines. In the later sixties, she also showed designs in metallic leather and snakeskin.

COLE: In the sixties, Cole of California's most exciting design was the "Scandal Suit" with its cutout sides and deep V-shaped neckline that extended below the waist. The theme of the collection was "New but not nude" as the cut-outs on Cole's bathing suits were filled with wide-mesh netting.

ANDRÉ COURRÉGES: In the early sixties, Courréges designed very short mini skirts and dresses in white and silver to be worn with high boots and goggles. His futuristic designs were referred to as "Space Age." He used contrasting colors on his trapeze dresses and trims. Courréges' late sixties designs were markedly softer, tending toward curves, rather than the angular look of his earlier collections. He showed knit catsuits and see-through and cut-out dresses.

LILLY DACHÉ: In the sixties, Lilly Daché designed cartwheel, lampshade, and pouf hats and feathered organdy coifs, tiny pillboxes, and space aged helmets.

OSCAR DE LA RENTA: Oscar de la Renta is known for his themed design collections that tend toward the outrageous. In the sixties, his collections were inspired by belle époque, abstract art, and oriental design. He used these themes in his cocktail dresses and beautiful ball gowns. In the late sixties, de la Renta also had a line of designs that were inspired by the youthful style of the hippies, with fringed ponchos, pants and vests. His designs for daywear included softly fitted cuts of mohair and wool with standaway collars and attenuated seams.

GALANOS: Galanos was known for his evening dresses and pantsuits. He favored a slim silhouette and used classical draping in chiffon, silks, cut velvet and brocades for his designs. He made intricate beaded embroidery decorations on his fashions and often used hand-painted silk prints by Raoul Dufy. In addition, Galanos designed pantsuits and pajama costumes.

RUDI GERNREICH: Gernreich was best-known for his sportswear separates and bathing suits in the sixties. He designed shirtwaist dresses, see-through blouses, and mini dresses with vinyl insets. His many bathing suit designs included the novel topless bathing suit for women with straps that went over the shoulder, attached to the waist at front and back. In 1964, Gernreich worked for Warner's designing foundation styles that could adapt to the new backless, frontless, sideless fashions.

HUBERT GIVENCHY: In 1961, Givenchy designed Audrey Hepburn's costumes for the movie "Breakfast at Tiffany's."

HALSTON: It was not until 1966 that Halston began to design ready-to-wear fashions. He gained his reputation in the late sixties and early seventies as a designer of knitwear with a line of sweaters, wide-leg pants and turtlenecks. He designed simple clothing that clung to the body. Halston also used tie-dyed fabrics.

BETSEY JOHNSON: In the sixties, Betsey Johnson was a young designer who had a knack for youthful designs. Some of her most sensational designs included a clear vinyl dress that came with do-it-yourself stickers, silver motorcycle gear, noisy dresses with grommets at the hems, cowhide wrap mini skirts with thigh high boots, and dresses such as those worn by actress Julie Christie, with long, pointed collars.

LACOSTE: René Lacoste, a.k.a. "Le Crocodile," was a French tennis star of the twenties and early thirties, who started a business in the thirties selling short-sleeved, white shirts with a crocodile logo of his own design. These cotton shirts were worn widely in the sixties and seventies.

KARL LAGERFELD: In the late sixties, Lagerfeld designed mole, rabbit and squirrel fur coats and jackets which were dyed in bright colors. Other coat designs included reversible fur coats and leather and fabric jackets.

NORMAL NORELL: Norell's first collection of the sixties featured culotte walking skirts, harem pants and pantsuits with tailored silhouettes. He was known for his extravagant fabric choices for décolleté evening dresses, his sequin-covered sheath dress and his evening jumpsuit with calf-length knickers and sleeveless overcoat. In the late sixties, Norell showed several different lengths for dinner dresses: midi, floor-length and above-the-knee.

MARY QUANT: In the sixties, Mary Quant was known for her youthful and affordable clothing designs. She featured mini skirts, colored, opaque tights, skinny ribs and hip belts. In the late sixties, her designs were carried by J. C. Penney's.

YVES SAINT LAURENT: Yves Saint Laurent's first collection of the sixties showed gold buttoned navy pea jackets and workmen's smocks in jersey, silk and satin. Later designs included thigh-high boots, Mondrian-inspired color block dresses, tuxedo jackets for women and velvet knickers.

SCAASI: In the sixties, Scaasi designed evening gowns and clothes for custom order. He used outré materials for his designs such as aluminum colored cellophane and sheer silk covered with huge sequins. His gowns relied on simple but well-cut shapes and helped their wearers make striking entrances.

c. 1962 Sally Victor white wool felt hat appliquéd with blue, orange and black, inspired by the paintings of Piet Mondrian. Courtesy of the Philadelphia Museum of Art. Given by Miss Rubye Graham.

JACQUES TIFFEAU: In the late fifties, when Tiffeau began designing independently, his specialty was sportswear. His sixties designs also tended toward more casual activity. In the mid-sixties, Tiffeau designed boxy jacket and tight pant ensembles. Other designs included heavily sculpted garments of wool and cotton, Western-style skirts with squared armholes, suits and other designs in corduroy, wide plaid wools and silks. In the late sixties, Tiffeau designed jersey dresses with empire waists, which were worn with thigh-high boots and long skirts.

VALENTINO: Valentino was an Italian designer known for elegant, tasteful designs.

SALLY VICTOR: Sally Victor was a premier milliner whose couture designs could cost as much as $1,000 a piece when they included fur and jewels. Some of her other sixties designs included striped berets, patent leather visors and floppy organza hats. Her less expensive designs were sold under the "Sally V" label.

JOHN WEITZ: In the sixties, Weitz designed fashions for men.

THE 1970s
LOGOS & LABELS

The riotous ways of the sixties were still apparent in the early seventies as women went from elephant pants to midis to hot pants. Finally, women rejected all these designs and opted for natural styles in tailored pants and pantsuits. Fashion model Lauren Hutton typified the natural look with her blow dry hairstyle, natural makeup and simple gold chain jewelry. Women began careers outside of the home and needed clothing suitable for the workplace. It was also a time when dressing meant prominently displaying the logos of four or five designers on clothing and accessories. Logos of fashion houses like Gucci, Chanel, Perry Ellis and Calvin Klein were competing for the fashion market.

One dress "uniform" was the pinstriped or vested pantsuit, styled after men's fashions. By 1976, women had adopted the man's tuxedo suit for evening. In 1977, Diane Keaton dressed in menswear with vest, tuxedo shirt, hacking jacket and fedora for the movie "Annie Hall." Natural

1971 Giorgio di Sant' Angelo original, lycra-antron white, green and purple parrot print leotard with purple skirt and green sash. Courtesy of Cedar Crest College Alumnae Museum, Allentown, PA. Photo by Tom Amico.

fabrics like silk, wool and cotton returned. Interest in ecology led to the prevalent use of earth tones in every aspect of designing, from home decorating to clothing. Leather returned as a popular material for handbags, briefcases, and shoes. The blazer, made popular by Bill Blass, was a staple in the wardrobe, as was the cotton jersey T-shirt dress. The long evening skirt in black, especially velvet, as well as tartan plaid, remained popular throughout the decade. Sometimes a blazer was added to create an evening suit. Designer jeans were snug and acceptable for dressy occasions. Exercise was popular and the leotard appeared originally for workouts, but later in clothing designs worn with pants and skirts. The string bikini was a new swimsuit addition.

Calvin Klein received three Coty awards in the seventies for his separates, all based on finely tailored silhouettes. Ethnic fashion was also a trend. In 1976, Yves Saint Laurent created "Russian" fashions, followed by his Chinese collection inspired by President Richard M. Nixon's trip to China. Japanese designer Kenzo Takada added to Western dress accents like kimono sleeves, shawls and layered looks. Giorgio di Sant' Angelo designed clothing with ethnic influences, such as the peasant-style caftan. Ralph Lauren showed the "prairie look" toward the end of the decade. Laura Ashley began designing textiles for the home and later developed an English country dress style.

Boutiques in department stores featured the labels of less expensive designers, and couture was not the only influence on styles. Millinery and couture departments closed. Women had their own ideas about dress. Fashion designers such as Zandra Rhodes showed punk designs which helped make an anti-fashion style fashionable. Ready-to-wear manufacturers were able to produce a variety of clothing that met women's fashion needs. Another factor in the decreasing role of couturiers was that many of the great early designers such as Chanel, Balenciaga, Schiaparelli, Vionnet and Norell died in the seventies, leaving serious voids along with their legacies.

Women were creating their own personal style of dress. "Retro" mania created interest in vintage clothing and auction houses began selling antique and vintage clothing. Platform cork espadrilles was another "retro" item for women.

The tailored styles of the seventies would be replaced by the affluent eighties. Younger designers moved to the forefront. The eighties were filled with fashions reminiscent of many traditional modes of dress. A desire for status symbols and big spending brought back excess in fashion, but also provided more choice. Princess Diana brought back formality to dress and Donna Karan brought femininity to work clothes.

In the early seventies, men's fashions went wide, especially lapels and ties. Ties reached a record five inches across. Flowered and psychedelic ties and bow ties in cotton fabrics were favorites. Bold striped or patterned dress shirts with long pointed collars were worn with polyester knit suits. Knit trousers were also very popular, with back buckle western pockets and flared pant legs. Flared trousers were accented by blunt toe shoes or Frye boots. Men wore their hair long with big sideburns. The constant question was, "Is it a girl or a boy?" as long, straight hair was now fashionable for both sexes and unisex clothing like body-tight, ribbed turtlenecks and flared pants were the trend. In place of a shirt and tie under jackets, many men were wearing turtlenecks.

Italian designer Armani was one of the only couture designers who first designed men's fashions, followed by a collection for women. He designed soft clothing and was known for tweeds on tweeds. Other designers like Pierre Cardin and Ralph Lauren designed for men as well. At the close of the seventies, men's fashions evolved to a more individualized mode of dress. The eighties offered more variety and color with many "retro" influences and interesting fabric choices.

Important Designers and Manufacturers of the 1970s

ADOLFO: In the seventies, Adolfo featured clean-lined knit designs, such as crocheted halter dresses and Chanel-inspired suits in bouclée yarns.

GIORGIO ARMANI: Armani began his career as a menswear' designer. He is, perhaps, most famous for his men's suits; however, his later designs for women share the same understated style of these suits. One of his most influential designs of the seventies was his loose-cut blazers.

LAURA ASHLEY: In the 1970s, Ashley began to use an Edwardian style with high collars and leg-of-mutton sleeves. Most of her fabrics were floral motifs inspired by textile designs of the eighteenth and nineteenth centuries.

GEOFFREY BEENE: Beene's designs of the early seventies were similar to his wool dresses with collars and cuffs from the sixties. In the late seventies, he showed a generous, skirted look on pants, jumpsuits and pajamas. In addition to his couture line, Beene had less expensive collections under the names Beene Bazaar, Beene Boutique and Beene Bag.

BILL BLASS: Bill Blass's best-known design of the seventies was his single-breasted blazer with a single button. He showed these jackets with pants. Blassport was his less expensive line.

STEPHEN BURROWS: In the mid-seventies, Stephen Burrows was known for his daring fashion designs: leather clothes decorated with studded nails, disco fashions in matte jersey, and garments of jersey with zig-zag stitching and lettuce edges.

PIERRE CARDIN: In 1970, Pierre Cardin's belted, cardigan suit for men helped promote more casual suited look. His women's fashions were known for their strong lines and uncomplicated quality.

BONNIE CASHIN: In the seventies, Cashin started the Knittery which produced her handmade sweater designs. She showed short and long dresses, long skirts unbuttoned over pants and tunics over leggings. She also designed leather purses.

HOUSE OF CHANEL: suit, gilt chain purse and pearls.

LIZ CLAIBORNE: In the mid-seventies, when Liz Claiborne first began to design independently, she strived to meet the demands of working women who needed moderately-priced clothing for work and leisure.

OSSIE CLARK: British designer Ossie Clark featured classic seventies styles: hot pants, maxi coats, handkerchief point hemlines on long dresses and skirts, and wrap-around dresses which exposed part of the back.

OSCAR DE LA RENTA: Whether from his couture or ready-to-wear collections for women, Oscar de la Renta's day and evening designs were bright and upbeat in the seventies. As in the sixties, his most renowned designs were cocktail dresses and ball gowns. Many of these evening dresses had flounced skirts and fitted bodices with cummerbunds at the waist. He used a variety of fabrics in solids and prints, with patterns from Persian rug designs.

FRYE: Frye was a popular company which manufactured boots in the seventies.

GUCCI: In the seventies, Gucci accessories, especially purses and scarves, which appeared earlier, were coveted by the label-conscious consumer.

HALSTON: Halston's most well-known seventies design was the halter-top dress that clung from the body to the ankles. He had several other dress designs in the seventies including cashmere dresses, loose-fitting caftan-style dresses and strapless, long dresses with a sarong tying over the breasts.

CATHY HARDWICK: Cathy Hardwick was known in the seventies for her affordable separates, designed to coordinate with previous years' collections.

BETSEY JOHNSON: In the seventies, Betsey Johnson was best known for her stretchy designs of matte jersey for disco dancing. Other designs sported her signature spirit, including brightly colored knits, high-waisted, hip-hugger pants and Princess style dresses. She also created bathing suits, retro sundresses and off-the-shoulder tops with leggings.

NORMA KAMALI: Norma Kamali first established herself in the seventies with her quilted coats of nylon and down. Her second most popular collection used sweatshirt material for pants, jackets, shirts and short cheerleader skirts. In the mid and late seventies, Kamali showed suits and silk dresses and wrap bathing suits that were all one piece.

ANNE KLEIN: In the seventies, Anne Klein was known for her sportswear designs, including wasp-waisted dresses, blazers and battle jackets. Her separates with their well-cut lines were very popular throughout the decade: hooded blouson tops, jersey dresses, bodysuits with zipped on mini skirts, kilts and knickers. In 1972, Anne Klein died but her house continues to create designs.

CALVIN KLEIN: In the early seventies, Calvin Klein showed sportswear collections which included coatdresses, jumpsuits, his famous blazer pantsuits, tank tops and shirt jackets. His sportswear was known for its clean lines and soft tailoring. In the late seventies, Klein's designs became increasingly sophisticated with slim line coats, loosely cut jackets and blazers, and linen and silk designs. His designer jeans took off in the late seventies and remained very popular into the eighties.

RALPH LAUREN: Ralph Lauren's seventies collections were inspired by English country fashion with hacking jackets and hunting clothes. His other collections included women's suits with men's style tailoring, Fair Isle sweaters, pleated skirts, walking shorts and trench coats. In 1974, he created the costume designs in linen for the movie "The Great Gatsby." In the late seventies, Ralph Lauren came out with his "prairie look" design denim skirt over a petticoat.

KARL LAGERFELD FOR CHLOE: In the mid-seventies, when designing for Chloe, Karl Lagerfeld showed shepherdess-style dresses with scarves tied around the torso and waist to form a bodice.

BOB MACKIE: In the seventies, Bob Mackie was best known for his floor-length evening dresses worn by Carol Burnett and Cher on their respective television shows.

MARY McFADDEN: In the mid-seventies, Mary McFadden was established as an independent company. The house's first collection included charmeuse robes with one shoulder and quilted vests with Chinese decoration. Other collections included Fortuny-style silks for dresses with hand-painted or quilted patterns in international motifs. Throughout the decade, however, McFadden was best known for her quilted coats and jackets with Middle Eastern, oriental or African designs.

ZANDRA RHODES: In the seventies, Zandra Rhodes was known for her avant-garde designs. Rhodes's designs often used hand-screened chiffons and silks for interesting evening dresses with uneven hemlines. Rhodes used art deco motifs, zig zag patterns, as well as designing her own prints featuring large lipsticks or cacti. In the late seventies, she brought punk into high fashion with her pink dresses which featured gold pins and gold embroidered holes.

YVES SAINT LAURENT: In the early seventies, Yves Saint Laurent was best known for his signature blazers. In the mid-seventies, he showed peasant-inspired collections with bodices and long, full skirts, worn with boots. He also designed a line of tailored clothes for female executives.

GIORGIO DI SANT' ANGELO: In the seventies, Sant' Angelo designed innovative clothing of stretchy jersey. He showed leotards, bodysuits, and dresses with wrap skirts in this material with bright, bold patterned prints. He created western-Navaho and gypsy-inspired lines in the seventies as well. Later, he designed more sophisticated lines for female executives.

SCAASI: During the seventies, Scaasi designed luxurious formal clothes, such as hand-painted crepe de chine caftans. His specialty, however, continued to be evening dresses with small, fitted waists and full skirts. Many of his designs used expensive bugle beading and some came with coordinating jewelry.

KENZO TAKEDA: Kenzo Takeda brought exciting innovations to United States' designers with his full, deep kimono-style sleeves and squared shoulders in his knitwear collection of separates and shawls.

*1971 Giorgio di Sant'
Angelo silk cream dress
with faux pony trim,
matching hot pants, and
suede belt with shell buckle.* Courtesy of Cedar Crest
College Alumnae Museum,
Allentown, PA.
Photo by Tom Amico.

VALENTINO: In the seventies, Valentino continued to design elegant clothes for evening, with dramatic details.

DIANE VON FURSTENBERG: Diane Von Furstenberg's most popular design of the seventies was her mid-length wrap dress in geometric and floral printed jersey. Her wrap-around dresses had long sleeves and closely fitted tops.

SPECIAL INTERESTS:
CHILDREN'S FASHIONS

Children's clothing is saved more often by families than any other garment. Parents treasure these pieces which are often passed along to succeeding generations, especially for special celebrations or holidays.

Early nineteenth century christening robes and bonnets were beautifully ornamented with embroidered lace. They came in a variety of styles, including the high waist empire style which is still the traditional modern design for such robes. Victorian heirlooms were made of lace, tucks and embroidery on the yoke. Silk underslips and bonnets with rosettes and fine ribbon ties were made to match the robes. Later, family members often made baby bonnets with tatting, lace or embroidery.

A variety of suit styles was designed for boys and girls in the nineteenth and early twentieth centuries. Probably the best known is the sailor suit with matching large crowned caps, bloused tops and pants or skirts. These were made popular by the British royal family. A popular suit for boys which is often captured in photographs is the Lord Fauntleroy suit with velvet tunic, wide lace collar and cuffs, and a wide sash tied over knickerbockers. Hair was long and curled, and feathered hats completed the outfit. In some photographs, young boys were shown in skirts which was considered acceptable dress into the early 1900s.

The Eton suit, a popular turn-of-the-century style for boys, had a Norfolk jacket, high starched shirt and wide black bow at the neck, with knickerbockers and knee socks.

Victorian girls were dressed in pantaloons, which showed under their pinafored skirts. Such styles were captured by Kate Greenaway, an English author and illustrator who popularized fashions for children in the late nineteenth century. High waist, ruffled yokes and big collars were typical Kate Greenaway designs that were revived into the 1940s.

The low-waisted dress of broderie anglaise, with ribbon sashes and beautifully created bonnets, were especially typical of the fancy clothing of the Edwardians. Clothing was made from starched white cotton, lawn, and cotton pique.

Twentieth–century children's clothing became simpler, mirroring changing adult fashions and attitudes. Short dresses with belts at the hips were worn in the early 1900s. Jeanne Lanvin made "Lanvin Blue" popular in 1914 when she began designing clothing for her daughter. In the 1920s,

c. 1920 emerald green silk velvet child's dress appliquéd with burgundy, blue and pink ribbon flowers with embroidery and mother of pearl buttons. Courtesy of Marianna Klaiman, Waldwick, NJ. Photo by Tom Amico.

appliqué work was done on simple dresses. Liberty & Co. offered smocked dresses in the early twentieth century. In the 1930s, the "Shirley Temple" dress with short puffed sleeves and above–the–knee length was the rage. Handknitted cardigans and polo necked sweaters came into vogue for children in the 1930s as well. In the 1930s and 1940s previous party wear was dressed up by adding lace collars and cuffs. Formal party dresses were full-skirted in taffetas and velvets. Ribbons, ruching and embroidery, as well as the well-known petticoat, were additional trimming for girls' dresses in the late 1940s and 1950s. Long party dresses came into vogue with the "New Look." In 1950, the Princess style dress was another fashion choice. For boys, tartan plaids and short pants with high socks returned.

Clothing designers created styles for children as well as for women. Claire McCardell designed mother/daughter fashions in the forties. Betsey Johnson designed clothing for children in the late sixties and early seventies.

In the past, straw hats were a fashion accessory for girls, whether a sailor style with streamers or with floral trim. Poke bonnets gave way to wide brims in the 1930s. Assorted berets and felt hats were also worn. In the seventies, old-fashioned sun hats with brims and flowers and granny gowns were revitalized in fashions for children.

Today, there is a wide selection of children's clothing. Early party dresses still have the charm of a bygone era and are often reproduced in modern fabrics. Finding a beautiful vintage piece with handwork and fine fabric that is no longer manufactured is a wonderful addition to a collection.

BRIDAL DESIGNS

Bridal dress usually reflected current trends in fashion as well as styles of royal weddings or those of prominent personalities of the time.

Napoleon's marriage to Eugenie in 1852 had an enormous impact on what was considered fashionable. Eugenie's dresses encouraged the use of the crinoline cage worn under the garment. Women's skirts reached huge proportions; sumptuous fabrics were used at court and were beautifully displayed on large full skirts. Eugenie's gowns were made by

Point de gaze lace wedding veil given by Mrs. William H. Vanderbilt to her grandaughter in 1895. At one time accompanied a satin gown from The House of Worth. One lace expert estimated it may have taken four or more years to make. Courtesy of Karen Augusta, North Westminster, VT.

couturier Charles Worth and rarely did she wear a gown twice. These very expensive couture gowns were as beautifully made inside as out and embellished with distinctive trims. Beautiful laces were greatly prized. An example of this style is a veil in point de gaze, given by Mrs. William H. Vanderbilt to her granddaughter for her wedding in 1895. The bridal gown with which it was worn was designed by the House of Worth, much in keeping with the last three decades of the nineteenth century when affluent American women looked to Paris to order Worth wedding gowns.

By 1860, a plaid silk taffeta wedding dress was favored over solid colors or white. Throughout this period there were various solid color wedding dresses as well. Country women would wear their wedding dress as a best dress after the wedding, and so solid was a more practical choice than a pattern which might be quickly outdated. The addition of the bustle in the Victorian gown was another trend women followed with their wedding gown designs. President Grant's eighteen-year-old daughter was married in the White House in 1874, wearing a decorative silk, tiered skirted gown with bustle and petticoat.

Black was an acceptable color for wedding dresses throughout the nineteenth century. Other trends were the unusual white gown in 1870, with the Victorian addition of the white veil of purity. Lace fans were part of a bride's attire in Victorian and Edwardian times. By 1900, the proper wedding outfit included dresses made from white or ivory organdy, cotton, sheer linen, lawn or silk. The full front bodice was ornamented in great detail with tucks, ribbons, eyelet and lace, characteristic of Edwardian fashion. Embroidered veils and trains accompanied gowns. The bride's trousseau was equally full of lace and embroidery.

By 1915, wedding gowns had a straighter skirt and a more natural shape. The underclothing of the bride had also changed. Without severe corseting, gowns were simpler with straight lines. In the

1907 Edwardian wedding portrait of bride and groom Freida and William Koch. Note aigrette on bride's headpiece and groom's white waistcoat. Photo courtesy of Jane Kiernan, Ridgewood, NJ.

mid-1920s, low-waisted short skirts, just below the knee, were in vogue with a floor length veil and/or train. The bridesmaids of the 1920s, in contrast, often wore full-length dresses.

Thirties' brides, influenced by Hollywood fashions, demanded the elegance of a full length, or uneven hemmed gown and yards of tulle. The beautiful bias-cut silk gown worn by Claudette Colbert in the movie, "It Happened One Night," was a lovely example of the thirties style bride. A black satin wedding gown made a brief appearance in this decade, with the bride carrying a calla lily.

Even war time restrictions on the use of clothing materials made an exception for wedding dresses. The sweetheart neckline was used on many forties wedding gowns. Artificial silk or rayon were commonly used for bridal dresses. Hollywood designers dressed Katharine Hepburn in a classic forties gown with shoulder pads and cummerbund for the 1942 movie, "Woman of the Year."

The 1950s typified the Dior look. It was a time of affluence, and even a modest gown had regality with beautiful lace or embroidery. The wedding of the decade was that of Princess Grace, whose gown

1912 off-white satin wedding gown with net lace overskirt and drape of machine-made Valenciennes lace with straight train to the floor. Courtesy of Cedar Crest College Alumnae Museum, Allentown, PA. Photo by Tom Amico.

1953 strapless, tiered wedding gown with scalloped neck and matching jacket. Courtesy of Cedar Crest College Alumnae Museum, Allentown, PA. Photo by Tom Amico.

was designed by Hollywood's Helen Rose and is in the costume collection of The Philadelphia Museum of Art. It was the most extravagant of any bridal gown of the time, with petticoats, Valenciennes lace and pearls.

Tiered strapless gowns were also part of the fifties fashion. Some gowns had feather boning and Elizabethan collars. Many were ballerina-length, and some brides wore tiaras. Later in the decade, and into the sixties, the sheath influenced the design of the wedding dress.

In the sixties, bridal fashions were most influenced by the style of Jackie Kennedy; a princess sleeveless straight style with pillbox headpiece, the style of the decade. The paper wedding dress was a fad of the times and the mini-skirted wedding gown was the exception. Often, the new nylon fabric Quiana was used to give the illusion of silk. Hairpieces and wigs often took the place of headpieces.

The seventies saw many types of wedding gowns as women began to look for individual expression in choosing wedding apparel. The most popular look was the romantic or granny gown with picture hats. Ethnic wedding dresses were another popular trend.

The royal marriage of Princess Diana in the eighties encouraged many brides to consider a more elaborate and traditional wedding dress than the previous two decades. Lady Diana's gown was designed by David and Elizabeth Emanuel, renowned for the off-the-shoulder bouffant style, and full-skirted silk taffetas with tulle and velvet. Throughout the affluent eighties, therefore, formal weddings were prevalent.

Today's brides choose from many wedding fashions. Designer bridal gowns reflect any number of fashion periods in history as well as unadorned contemporary styling. There are always brides who favor wearing an heirloom gown or veil. Although modern brides have more choices than any other time, the twentieth century bride has traditionally favored a white or ivory dress, formal in nature, with hat or veil.

WESTERN STYLES

The American cowboy of 1890 wore a Stetson hat, a bandanna, wool or cotton shirt, vest with pockets, gloves or gauntlets of deerskin, chaps, and boots. Fringed gauntlets were beaded in bright colors with tooled work often displayed on the gauntlet. The chaps were seatless leg coverings needed for protection. Each cowboy had his own favorite style of Stetson hat, adding a personal crease in the crown. Favorite cowboy hats had wide shade brims, high crowns and were gray or brown in color.

Early movies which featured authentic cowboy garb made Western wear popular in the East. Later, the interest in dude ranches further popularized Western wear and John Wayne's movies of the thirties added an element of glamour. Two-tone sateen shirts with buttons and flaps were popular in this decade. Later, shirts in gabardine, rayon, cotton or wool were manufactured. The hatbands were made of silk or were beaded.

In the forties, cowboy and Western scenes were reproduced on ties, reflecting interest in the cowboy's life. The photo tie and handpainted tie were both designed with Western motifs.

There are several well-known designers of the Western shirt. Nathan Turk in Los Angeles made embroidered shirts. Rodeo Ben, a Philadelphia designer of Western wear, produced shirts with mother-of-pearl snaps in the thirties, forties and fifties. He supplied many of the television cowboys with their clothing, especially Gene Autry. Viola Grae, another Western designer, added jewel and embroidery work to clothing. Nudies brand of Western wear was made in California, primarily for the movies.

With the popularity of television Westerns in the fifties, featuring stars like Roy Rogers and Dale Evans, Western clothing appeared in clothing stores everywhere. H-bar-C and California Ranch Wear were popular brands. Children's Western outfits were popular at this time as well.

Western fashions also encompass Native American wear as well. Native American clothing includes Navajo skirts, authentic pouches, moccasins, beaded shirts and bags.

Western fashions have inspired current fashion designers at different times. Ralph Lauren's popular country Western jeans, jean skirts, cowboy boots and prairie skirts are reminiscent of the Old West. Jeans, a truly American style of dress, have remained a part of twentieth century American fashion.

THINK & TALK LIKE AN EXPERT

CHAPTER 2

COLLECTORS' CRITERIA

If you keep in mind the following criteria, you will not only sound like a "pro," but are more likely to avoid costly mistakes.

CONDITION: The condition of a garment or fabric is of utmost importance. A small tear can be just the beginning of something larger. It is necessary to inspect a selection with a keen eye. Look for repairs as well. Often, they have not been made in the best interest of the fabric and undoing them can be costly and is not always successful. How a fabric has been cared for is a very important consideration before investing your time and money. Small but interesting scraps can be salvaged if there is embroidery or other handiwork. Check for stitching and stains. Ask if the garment has been cleaned in any way. A garment in mint condition will naturally mandate that a collector pay a higher price but this could be a better decision in the long run.

CONSERVATION AND RESTORATION GUIDELINES: Knowing how to properly store and care for your vintage clothing and fabrics is important. Experts agree the hardest conditions for fabric to endure are light and dirt. Dry cleaning for most fabrics should be avoided whenever possible unless the garment was more recently made. Almost all garments can be shaken or dusted lightly with a Dustbuster to remove dust and light dirt if special care is taken to safeguard trim and buttons. Small cottons and linens that have been tested for color-fastness can be soaked in a bath of lukewarm water to which sodium perborate has been added. Extra care must be given to ensure that the water weight will not damage the cloth when it is lifted from the basin. The water must be changed and fresh water added as the dirt loosens. Usually, conservators use a piece of unbleached muslin to support large pieces. Always do the final rinse in distilled water to prevent impurities from remaining in the fabric and damaging it. Drying can be done by spreading the fabric or garment on towels to dry. Do not wring any garment. Always remember to treat vintage fabric "with kid gloves." Silk is sometimes washable, but one should be very careful since it often depends on how and where the garment was made. Satin shatters with age and special precautions should be taken when handling and storing it. Dresses with linings should be treated as two separate pieces since they often require different types of attention.

The beauty of vintage pieces lies in their uniqueness and design. However, a poorly repaired garment only magnifies the mistake. It is, therefore, better to accept it as a lovely antique, as you would any vintage object. A list of suggested conservators apears at the end of this book in *The Vintage Fashion & Fabric Collectors' Resource Guide*. The guide lists people who have studied the history and care of clothing and fabrics. They have proved invaluable in discerning the proper steps to be taken with regard to a piece.

When storing vintage clothing and fabrics, invest in acid-proof tissue paper for wrapping. Avoid hanging clothing, which puts extra weight on the garment and results in tearing, especially in the shoulders. If a hanger is used even briefly, only use a well-padded one. Acid-free boxes can be ordered through conservation suppliers; however, they can be expensive for the average collector, particularly if you plan to collect many pieces. In any event, always use a clean box with a fitted lid to keep out dirt and light. Hat boxes are good for storing hats since they prevent them from being crushed. Newspapers can be used in your storage area to prevent insect infestation as long as they do not touch the garments. Never rely on mothballs or plastic bags for storage. Store boxes away from extremes in temperature or dampness.

ESSENTIAL VOCABULARY: You should become familiar with all the terms associated with your vintage pieces. The history sections and glossary of this book will assist you in developing a valuable, working vocabulary. Always feel free to ask an antique dealer about the background of a vintage piece—where it came from and how it was used. Asking questions and examining pieces is the fastest way to expand your knowledge of vintage fashion and fabrics.

HOW TO BUY & SELL: We strongly recommend attending shows to learn more about vintage fashion and fabrics. Show promoters are listed in *The Fashion & Fabrics Collectors' Resource Guide* at the end of this book, which will help you locate shows in your area. Many are specialized for clothing and textiles. There is a substantial amount of merchandise at shows that will give you an idea of what is being bought and sold. This can often lead to a better understanding of the value of your own collection. Shops that specialize in vintage fashion are also listed in *The Vintage Fashion & Fabrics Collectors' Resource Guide* and can be a valuable resource. It is impossible to learn everything you need to know in one day, but you can feel confident about making a great deal of progress through observation alone.

What if you want to sell a piece in you collection? First, you must learn more about what you have. Take the time to refer to a guidebook. The more knowledge you have of an item (date, design, condition), the better informed you will be of its value. With this information, you can go to dealers, see what they may have that is similar, and ask what they think the market value would be for such an item. Most dealers love to talk to collectors about their favorite subject. After you have an idea of the value, ask dealers what they would pay for the item. Remember, the dealer is going to have to resell your piece, so the offer will not be the market price. Dealers cannot pay for sentimental value either. Be sure it is something you want to sell. Dealers will be interested that it was "grandma's", but they will not factor sentimented value into the price. It is important to remember that dealers do not always have a customer in mind or need a particular item. In that case, it may be worthwhile to ask if they know someone who might be interested.

MARKET TRENDS: Pricing fluctuates with fads. However, a good quality, mint condition piece and one of historical importance, whether by its label or design, is always valuable. In clothing and accessories couture, designer labels will demand high prices. Where you buy or sell is also important. Larger cities demand higher prices. Something you find at a flea market will not be the same price, hopefully, that you will pay in a shop or at a quality show. The best insurance in determining the value of an item to buy or sell is knowledge. Again, try to learn as much as you can. When buying any vintage piece, buy primarily for beauty—fabric, design and fine workmanship—and you will not be disappointed.

KEY WORDS TO REMEMBER

There are five important terms you need to know to discuss vintage fashion and fabrics.

1. **Style:** Does the item of reference have a "look?" For instance, does it have beautiful lines? Is it well made? Is there unusual detail or ornamentation? Does it incorporate design elements that work?

2. **Design:** Vintage clothing often embody important elements of good design, such as clear lines, quality of structure, color and texture. There are many things that influence the design of a garment. Knowing what inspired the design (the designer, fabric, historic reference) helps in identification. The ability to recognize good design helps you to make good decisions when choosing garments to add to your collection.

3. **Structure:** How a garment, accessory or fabric is made is crucial to determining the age and/or quality of a piece.

4. **Material:** What is the piece in question made of or from? Is there more than one type of workmanship involved? Is the method of workmanship still used? Is the material still made?

5. **Quality:** Quality can never be underestimated. The thought in designing or the care given in workmanship will carry your vintage piece of fashion through many generations.

THE BASICS

In the excitement of finding and/or acquiring the "perfect" garment or accessory, even experienced dealers and collectors sometimes forget the basics. Keeping this list in mind is a good way to ensure you will have a collection you love for many years to come.

1. Choose vintage pieces with an eye for good design and/or fine workmanship.
2. Check clothing and accessories carefully for wear, tear and repairs before purchasing. Check for wear and tear particularly on the shoulders of silks or other fragile fabrics.
3. When shopping, have a tape measure handy for measuring clothing size and fabric length.
4. Follow proper cleaning and storage guidelines to maintain the condition of your vintage piece. See conservation guidelines given in the Collectors' Criteria (p. 109).
5. Always handle clothing, lace or fabric very carefully to avoid tears or breaks. Remember: the less handling, the better.
6. Before sewing vintage cotton fabrics, pre-wash them the same way you intend to wash the completed garment because they are not preshrunk fabrics.
7. Standardized sizing started in the forties as a result of fabric rationing during the war. Therefore, when buying clothes made earlier than 1940, sizes will vary greatly. Taking measurements is the best way to size a garment.
8. Always test spot a garment for color fastness and fabric condition before washing.
9. When in doubt about the care needed for your vintage piece, consult a conservator. Find suggested conservators listed in *The Vintage Fashion & Fabrics Collectors' Resource Guide.*
10. Look carefully for rust stains on whites and perspiration stains on all clothing before you purchase because they are not easy to remove.

VINTAGE FASHION & FABRICS COLLECTORS' RESOURCE GUIDE

CHAPTER 3

MUSEUMS, SOCIETIES AND ORGANIZATIONS

The museums listed below house nationally known collections that are very extensive. In many cases, individuals with research interests may make an appointment to see the holdings; most also have rotating displays.

ARIZONA

The Phoenix Art Museum
Arizona Costume Institute
(a predominantly Western collection)
1625 North Central Avenue
Phoenix, AZ 85004
(602) 257-1222

CALIFORNIA

Los Angeles County Museum
Costume and Textile Department
5905 Wilshire Boulevard
Los Angeles, CA 90036
(213) 937-4250

M. H. de Young Memorial Museum
Golden Gate Park
San Francisco, CA 94118
(415) 558-2887

The Oakland Museum
1000 Oak Street
Oakland, CA 94607
(415) 273-3842

CONNECTICUT

Wadsworth Atheneum
600 Main Street
Hartford, CT 06103
(203) 278-2670

ILLINOIS

The Art Institute of Chicago
Michigan Avenue at Adams Street
Chicago, IL 60603
(312) 443-3600

Chicago Historical Society
Clark Street at North Avenue
Chicago, IL 60614
(312) 642-4600

MASSACHUSETTS

The Museum of Fine Arts
465 Huntington Avenue
Boston, MA 02115
(617) 267-9300

NEW YORK

Brooklyn Museum
Eastern Parkway
Brooklyn, NY 11238
(718) 638-5000

Cooper-Hewitt Museum
Smithsonian Museum of Design
2 East 91st Street
New York, NY 10128
(212) 860-6868

The Fashion Institute of Technology
The Edward C. Blum Design Laboratory
227 West 27th Street
New York, NY 10001
(212) 760-7708

Metropolitan Museum of Art
Costume Institute
Fifth Avenue at 82nd Street
New York, NY 10028
(212) 879-5500, extension 3908/3909

Museum of the City of New York
Fifth Avenue at 103rd Street
New York, NY 10029
(212) 534-1672

OHIO
Cincinnati Art Museum
Eden Park
Cincinnati, OH 45202-1596
(513) 721-5204

Western Reserve Historical Society
The Chisholm Halle Costume Wing
10825 East Boulevard
Cleveland, OH 44106
(216) 721-5722

PENNSYLVANIA
Philadelphia Museum of Art
Benjamin Franklin Parkway, Box 7646
Philadelphia, PA 19101
(215) 763-8100

TEXAS
The Texas Fashion Collection
North Texas State University
Denton, TX 76203
(817) 565-2732

WASHINGTON
University of Washington
Historical Costume & Textile Collection
Seattle, WA 98195
(206) 543-1739

WASHINGTON, D.C.
The National Museum of American History
Smithsonian Institution
Constitution Avenue, between 12th & 14th Streets
Washington, D.C. 20560
(202) 357-3185 (Costume Division)

There are many small museums across the country
that house collections of local costumes on display.
Two examples are:

Cedar Crest College
Alumnae Museum
100 College Drive
Allentown, PA 18104
(610) 437-4471

The Hermitage
335 N. Franklin Turnpike
Ho-ho-kus, NJ 07423
(201) 445-8311

Museums of specialized interest are:

Hoguet Fan Museum and Atelier
2 boulevard Strasbourg
75010 Paris
33-1-42-08-19-89

The Glove Museum at LaCrasia
6 East 32nd Street, 6th Fl.
New York, NY 10016
(212) 532-1956
(by appointment)

VINTAGE CLOTHING AND TEXTILE SOCIETIES AND ORGANIZATIONS

The following societies and organizations offer memberships.

ENGLAND

The Fan Circle
24, Asmuns Hill
London, England NW116ET

INDIANA

International Old Lacers, Inc.
2409 South Ninth Street
Lafayette, IN 47905

MARYLAND

The Costume Society of America
55 Edgewater Drive, P.O. Box 73
Earleville, MD 21919

NEW JERSEY

The Costume and Textile Group of New Jersey
P.O. Box 8623
Woodcliff Lake, NJ 07675

VINTAGE CLOTHING AND TEXTILE NEWSLETTER

Listed below are newsletters from societies and clubs around the nation that deal solely with issues of vintage clothing and textiles. To receive any of these publications, write to the address and request information.

Newsletters

CALIFORNIA
Vintage!
P.O. Box 412
Alamo, CA 94507
Vintage! is a publication of the Federation of Vintage Fashion which can be reached at the same address.

MASSACHUSETTS
The Echoes Report - "the newsletter for enthusiasts of the 1930s–1960s"
P.O. Box 2321
Mashpee, MA 02649
The Echoes Report is published by Deco Echoes Publications.

The Vintage Gazette
194 Amity Street
Amherst, MA 01002
The Vintage Gazette is a publication of Molly's Vintage Productions.

MISSOURI
The Lady's Gallery
P.O. Box 1761
Independence, MO 64055
This newsletter is not affiliated with any particular society or club.

NEW JERSEY
The Costume and Textile Group of New Jersey Newsletter
P.O. Box 8623
Woodcliff Lake, NJ 07675
This newsletter is a publication of The Costume and Textiles Group of N.J. and includes their programs as well.

OREGON
Vintage Clothing Newsletter
P.O. Box 1422
Corvalis, OR 97339
The Vintage Clothing Newsletter is an independent publication by Terry McCormick.

The Vintage Connection
904 North 65 Street
Springfield, OR 97478-7021
The Vintage Connection is produced by Pioneer Printworks and is not affiliated with any specific society, club or promoter.

MAGAZINES

The following magazines include vintage clothing and/or fabrics in their publications. They may be found in newsstands, bookstores, or by subscription.

Ornament
P.O. Box 2349
San Marcos, CA
92079-2349
(800) 888-8950

Victoria
P.O. Box 7150
Red Oak, IA 51597
(800) 876-8696

Piecework
Interweave Press Inc.
201 East Fourth Street
Loveland, CO 80537
(303) 669-7672

STORES WHICH SPECIALIZE IN VINTAGE FASHION AND FABRICS

The following stores specialize in vintage fashion and fabrics

CALIFORNIA

Stop the Clock
2140 Center Street
Berkeley, CA 94704
(510) 841-2142
Stop the Clock carries both men's and women's clothing and accessories from the 1940s through the 1960s. They also have a special collection of Hawaiian shirts.

Faded Glory
141 Yale Street
Claremont, CA 91711
(909) 625-0083
Faded Glory carries both men's and women's vintage clothing. They specialize in Levis and leather jackets.

Vintage Silhouettes
1301 Pomona Street
Crockett, CA 94525
(510) 787-7274
Vintage Silhouettes carries

men's, women's and children's "wearable" fashions and accessories from the 1860s through the 1950s. In addition, they carry a collection of Edwardian and Victorian fashions.

The Butler's Cottage
1187 Beach Park Blvd.
Foster City, CA 94404
(415) 341-6979
FAX (415) 341-3453
The Butler's Cottage has an inventory of fashions from 1915–1935, but specializes in items from the 1920s & 1930s. They also carry an extensive collection of wedding gowns, beaded gowns, head pieces, silk lingerie and silk stockings.

Cadillac Jack's
2820 Gilroy
Hollywood, CA 90039
(800) 775-5078
Featured in People magazine,

Cadillac Jack's carries vintage Western fashion and benchmade boots. Specializing in men's clothing, they also carry hand-painted vintage neckties and Hawaiian shirts.

The Lundberg Haberdashery

396 Colusa Avenue
Kensington, CA 94707
(510) 524-3003

The Lundberg Haberdashery exclusively carries mens' suits, separates, hats and shoes from 1850 to 1950. Some of their specialties include thirties and forties Palm Beach brand suits, a large inventory of thirties and forties neckties, tuxedos, gabardine "Ike" jackets, and Borsolino hats.

Golyester

7957 Melrose Avenue
Los Angeles, CA 90046
(213) 655-3393

Golyester carries women's fashions and accessories from the late 1800s through the 1950s. Among their specialties are women's suits from the 1930s and 1940s, hats from the 1920s to the 1950s, ethnic fashions from the late 1800s, and Spanish and Chinese shawls. They also carry an extensive inventory of textiles, ribbons, buttons, and trims.

Playback

622 N. Doheny Drive
Los Angeles, CA 90069
(310) 273-5673

Playback carries women's and children's clothing, fabrics, and laces. Their specialty is white, lace dresses from 1900 through the 1930s.

Repeat Performance

318 North LaBrea Ave.
Los Angeles, CA 90036
(213) 938-0609

Repeat Performance carries mint condition fashions and accessories for men and women from the 1940s and 1950s.

Madame Butterfly

5474 College Avenue
Oakland, CA 94618
(510) 653-1525

With an inventory that covers the Victorian period through the 1970s, Madame Butterfly has women's clothing and accessories (hats, bags, jewelry, and shoes). They also rent costumes.

Reincarnation Antique Clothing

214 17th Street
Pacific Grove, CA 93950
(408) 649-0689

Reincarnation carries men's and women's clothing and accessories from the 1890s to the 1950s. They also have a special collection of antique silk kimonos.

Wear It Again Sam

3922 Park Boulevard
San Diego, CA 92103
(619) 299-0185

Wear It Again Sam carries mint condition, wearable men's and women's clothing from 1900–1950s, as well as hats, shoes, and purses. They specialize in Victorian and 1920s' wedding dresses.

Countess Olizar

1825 Polk Street
San Francisco, CA 94109
(415) 441-4930

A couture salon, Countess Olizar carries a fine collection of classic clothing from the twentieth century for men and women.

Pure Gold

625 State Street
Santa Barbara, CA 93101
(805) 962-4613

Pure Gold carries high quality, wearable men's and women's fashions and accessories from the 1920s through the 1960s. They also rent costumes.

Elizabeth Lucas
1021 Montana Avenue
Santa Monica, CA 90403
(310) 451-4058
Elizabeth Lucas carries clean, restored fashions for men and women from 1900 through the 1960s. Some of the many items include Victorian dresses, 1920s beaded gowns, lingerie, gabardine suits, and the occasional couture piece.

Paris 1900
2703 Main Street
Santa Monica, CA 90405
(310) 396-0405
Paris 1900 specializes in women's and children's fashion from the turn of the century through the 1930s. They also carry bridal pieces and do garment restoration work. Please call for an appointment.

Hot Couture
101 Third Street
Santa Rosa, CA 95401
(707) 528-7247
Covering 1900 through 1960, Hot Couture carries men's and women's wearable fashions and accessories. They also rent costumes.

CONNECTICUT

Roxie Taylor
Route 44, Avon Village
Avon, CT 06001
(203) 674-8917
Roxie Taylor's inventory includes men's and women's wearable vintage fashions from the turn of the century through the 1940s. They also carry vintage fabrics, lace and accessories.

Yesterday's Threads
564 Main Street
Branford, CT 06405
(203) 481-6452
Yesterday's Threads carries men's and women's clothing, accessories & costume jewelry from the 1800s through the 1940s.

Dud's Vintage Clothing & Jewelry Loft
10 Marietta Street
Hamden, CT 06514
(203) 248-8675
Dud's carries men's and women's fashions and antique and costume jewelry from the 1920s to the 1970s.

Retroactive
23 River Street
Milford, CT 06001
(203) 877-6050
Retroactive carries museum quality, wearable, classic couture from the 1920s through the late 1960s. They specialize in garments by Chanel.

Anne Marie's Vintage Boutique
869 Whalley Avenue
New Haven, CT 06515
(203) 387-2243
This boutique carries high quality antique pieces dating from 1840 to 1960. They specialize in beaded and mesh bags as well as embroidered shawls.

Casablanca
1219 Chapel Street
New Haven, CT 06511
(203) 789-1630
Casablanca has an inventory of lovely wearable clothing, accessories, lace and linens from the turn of the century to the 1960s.

FLORIDA

Creative Collections
527 South Pineapple Ave.
Sarasota, FL 34236
(813) 951-0477
Creative Collections carries men's and women's fashions from the Victorian period through the 1970s. They also have a special collection of bakelite and other costume jewelry.

ILLINOIS

Carrie's Vintage Clothing
204 North Neil
Champagne, IL 61820
(217) 352-3231
Carrie's is a large shop with a large inventory of wearable men's and women's fashions from the 1800s through the 1970s.

Renaissance Buttons
826 W. Armitage Avenue
Chicago, IL 60614
(312) 883-9508
Located in a beautiful Victorian house in the Lincoln Park neighborhood of Chicago, Renaissance Buttons carries a dazzling array of antique and vintage buttons. Their inventory includes 500,000 metal, plastic, celluloid, porcelain, rubber, horn, ivory, glass and jet buttons.

Adornments
125 W. Main Street
West Dundee, IL 60118
(708) 428-8323
Adornments specializes in women's vintage clothing from the 1930s, 1940s and 1950s. All their garments are clean and wearable.

The Victorian Emphasis
918 Green Bay Road
Winnetka, IL 60093
(708) 441-6675
Emphasizing pieces from 1820 to 1890, this shop carries an extensive collection of antique and vintage fashions, as well as textiles and fabrics. They also carry decorative accessories, shawls, needlepoint, and buttons. Their specialties are Edwardian whites, panné velvet caps and 1930s' gowns.

INDIANA

Red Rose Vintage Clothing
834 East 64th Street
Indianapolis, IN 46220
(317) 257-5016
Red Rose carries both men's and women's clothing from the 1940s and 1950s. They also have costume jewelry.

MASSACHUSETTS

Circa
42 Main Street
Fairhaven, MA 02719
(508) 997-9390
Circa deals in men's and women's wearable vintage clothing, as well as fabrics and lace. They also have period costumes.

"The Fainting Couch"
250 No. Main Street
Mansfield, MA 02048
(508) 339-7733
This lovely store specializes in fine, antique apparel & accessories from the Victorian era.

Beads and Buttons
2nd Floor, Thorne's Marketplace at 150 Main
Northampton, MA 01060
(413) 586-9517
Next door and related to the Northampton Fabric Co., Beads and Buttons carries a full selection of antique and vintage buttons. Their inventory includes buttons of bakelite, jet, metal and enamel. When available, they also have vintage beads, sequins and spangles.

The Northampton Fabric Co.
2nd Floor, Thorne's Marketplace at 150 Main
Northampton, MA 01060
(413) 585-0305
Professing to be "A garden of material delights," the

Northampton Fabric Co. offers antique fabrics by the yard, vintage trims, linens, scarves and shawls.

MISSOURI

Everybody's Everything
1523 Niles Avenue
St. Joseph, MI 49085
(616) 983-3276
With something for everyone, Everybody's Everything has men's and women's fashions from the Victorian period to the 1970s. They also rent costumes.

MINNESOTA

Lots O' Stuff
Mankato Place Mall
Mankato, MN 56001
(507) 345-3020
True to its name, Lots O' Stuff carries men's and women's fashions, fabrics, lace, buttons and trims from the 1970s and earlier. They also rent costumes.

MONTANA

Ragtime
332 1st Avenue W.
Kalispell, MT 59901
(406) 752-6638
Ragtime carries men's and women's wearable fashions and accessories from the 1920s through the 1960s. They carry authentic and costume jewelry and wrist watches. Their inventory of fabrics includes chintzes, bark cloth and fifties fabrics, all of which are sold by panel.

NORTH CAROLINA

The Victorian Lady
102 South Main Street
Waxhaw, NC 28173
1-800-786-1886
Dedicated to the fashions of Victorian ladies, this shop carries

predominantly women's fashions of that era. A catalog is available upon request.

NEW HAMPSHIRE

Antique Apparel
Box 1
Acworth, NH 03601
(603) 835-2295
Specializing in the eras between the Victorian period and the 1940s, Antique Apparel carries men's, women's, and children's fashions and accessories. Please call for an appointment.

NEW JERSEY

Time After Time
81 Main Street
Madison, NJ 07940
(201) 966-6877
Time After Time carries men's and women's fashions, designer clothes, and accessories from the turn of the century to the 1970s, as well as lace, buttons, and trims.

Incogneeto
164 Nassau Street
Princeton, NJ 08540
(609) 683-1181
Incogneeto and its sister store listed below carry men's and women's clothing from the 1950's and 1960's. With an extensive inventory of prom dresses, tuxes, costume jewelry and accessories, these stores have supplied costumes for many movies and plays. They also have a large collection of smoking jackets and kimonos.

Incogneeto
19 West Main Street
Somerville, NJ 07080
(908) 231-1887
The Somerville Incogneeto carries a similar inventory to the Princeton Incogneeto, so kindly read above.

NEW YORK
Metropolis
44 Central Avenue
Albany, NY 12206
(518) 427-2971
Metropolis specializes in men's and women's clothing, jewelry and accessories from 1850 through the 1960s. They also carry textiles and fabrics.

Red Balloons
42 Allen Street
Buffalo, NY 14202
(716) 881-2727
Red Balloons carries only museum quality, antique women's clothing, accessories, fabrics, fine lace, and trim from 1850 through 1930. Their specialties are early designer pieces and hats from the early teens and twenties.

Melange
1484 Hertle Avenue
Buffalo, NY 14216
(716) 838-9290
With an inventory covering the eras between 1800 and the 1960s, Melange has men's, women's, and children's clothing, as well as fabrics, lace, buttons, and trims.

Marilyn In Monroe
Route 17
Monroe, NY 10950
(914) 782-8757
Marilyn In Monroe carries men's and women's vintage fashions.

The Shoe Annex
20 First Avenue
New York, NY 10009
(212) 673-4532
The oldest vintage store in Manhattan, The Shoe Annex not only carries shoes from the 1940s through the 1970s, but clothing for both men and women. The Shoe Annex has sold costumes to movies and TV shows and privately rents costumes.

Alice Underground
481 Broadway
New York, NY 10007
(212) 431-9067
Alice Underground carries men's and women's fashions and accessories from the 1950s through the 1970s. They also have bins of fabrics and some designer pieces.

Cheap Jack's Vintage Clothing
841 Broadway
New York, NY 10023
(212) 995-0403
Carrying "everything from the turn of the century to modern times," Vintage Jack's has men's and women's clothing and accessories.

Dorothy's Closet
335 Bleecker Street
New York, NY 10014
(212) 206-6414
Dorothy's Closet carries men's and women's clothing and accessories from the 1930s through the 1960s. They have special collections of Hawaiian shirts and gabardine suits.

Jean Hoffman Antiques
236 East 80th Street
New York, NY 10021
(212) 535-6930
Jean Hoffman Antiques has a special collection of beautiful vintage wedding gowns, in addition to their inventory of decorative and antique fabrics and laces, accessories, and couture garments.

Lorraine Wohl Collection
150 East 70th Street
New York, NY 10021
(212) 472-0191
The Lorraine Wohl Collection specializes in women's clothing and couture, as well as accessories and jewelry. They also have a special collection of fine, beaded evening pieces.

O Mistress Mine
143 Seventh Avenue S.
New York, NY 10014
(212) 691-4327
In addition to their vintage fashion inventory that covers the turn of the century through the 1960s era, O Mistress Mine specializes in fancy deco and thirties gowns, and designer label pieces.

Panache Antiques
525 Hudson Street
New York, NY 10014
(212) 242-5115
Panache Antiques has a carefully collected inventory of clothing, textiles, and accessories from the 1900s to the 1950s.

Patricia Pastor
760 Madison Avenue
New York, NY 10021
(212) 734-4673
An exquisite and immaculate collection of couture and wearables, Patricia Pastor's inventory includes women's clothing and accessories from 1920 through 1960.

Schmul Meier, Inc. Antique Textiles
328 E. 59th Street, Suite 4
New York, NY 10022
(212) 644-8590
Schmul Meier carries only designer pieces of clothing, and American, Western and Eastern European fabrics from the seventeenth century to the 1950s.

Screaming Mimi's
382 Lafayette Street
New York, NY 10003
(212) 677-6464
Screaming Mimi's carries both men's and women's clothing and accessories as well as fabrics from the 1950s through the 1970s.

Star Struck
47 Greenwich Avenue
New York, NY 10011
(212) 691-5357
With specialties in Hawaiian shirts, suits and jackets and vintage blue jeans, Star Struck's inventory includes men's and women's clothing from the 1940s to the 1970s.

Star Struck
270 Bleecker Street
New York, NY 10011
(212) 366-9826
This Star Struck specializes in men's and women's fashions and accessories from the 1940s, 1950s and 1960s.

Tender Buttons
143 East 62nd Street
New York, NY 10021
(212) 758-7004
A wonderful little store, Tender Buttons has oodles of fascinating, unique buttons. They identify themselves as having the largest collection of antique and vintage buttons in America.

What Goes Around Comes Around
351 W. Broadway
New York, NY 10012
(212) 343-9303
An eclectic store open all hours in SoHo, What Goes Around Comes Around carries men's and women's fashions and accessories from the twentieth century. Their inventory includes everything from high end Victorian to 1960s' Sears polyester.

Silhouette
24 East Market Street
Rhinebeck, NY 12572
(914) 876-4545
In addition to their inventory of antique clothing. Silhouette specializes in antique textiles.

Piacente
38 Main Street
Tarrytown, NY 10591
(914) 631-4231
Piacente carries mostly 1940s and Victorian fashions for women as well as men's 1950s' fashions.

OHIO

Feather's Vintage Clothing
440 East 5th Street
Dayton, OH 45402
(513) 228-2940
Feather's specializes in the 1940s and 1950s. They carry men's and women's fashions and accessories, in addition to fabrics from those eras.

Talk of the Town
9019 Reading Road
Reading, OH 45215
(513) 563-8844
(513) 761-0344
Carrying mostly women's fashions, Talk of the Town has fashions from the 1800s through the 1970s. They also rent costumes.

PENNSYLVANIA

Petitpoints
Lahaska Antiques Center
Route 202
Lahaska, PA 18931
(215) 794-0343
Petitpoints specializes in fine vintage fashion for women as well as restored wedding dresses.

Wear It Again Sam
4430 Main Street
Manayunk, PA 19127
(212) 487-0525
A funky shop in a vintage garage, Wear It Again Sam is a great place to satisfy your urge for fifties fashions. They specialize in the 1940s through 1960s, and carry men's, women's and children's fashions and accessories.

Katy Kane, Inc.
34 West Ferry Street
New Hope, PA 18938
(215) 862-5873
Katy Kane carries fine ladies' garments from 1890 through 1945; however, their specialty is Victorian and Edwardian wedding gowns.

Maxie's Daughter
724 S. Fourth Street
Philadelphia, PA 19128
(215) 829-2226
Three store fronts full of vintage fabrics, with an extensive inventory of all fabrics sold by the yard.

SOUTH CAROLINA

Granny's Goodies
263 King Street
Charleston, SC 29401
(803) 577-6200
Granny's Goodies are men's and women's clothing from the 1890s to the present, especially tuxes and tails, and kimonos.

VIRGINIA

Side Show
1414 Colley Avenue
Norfolk, VA 23517
(804) 625-2264
Side Show carries clothing and accessories from 1930 to the 1950s.

Memory Makers
15 Middlebrook Avenue
Staunton, VA 24401
(703) 886-5341
Emphasizing the eras of the 1930s, 1940s and 1950s, Memory Makers carries men's and women's fashions and accessories, as well as lace and fabrics.

Echoes of Time
320–B Laskin Road
Virginia Beach, VA 23451
(804) 428-2332
Echoes of Time carries fashions and accessories for both men and women from the Victorian period through the 1950s. They also rent costumes.

VERMONT

Karen Augusta
31 Gage Street
North Westminster, VT
05101
(802) 463-4958
For the serious collector, by appointment only, Karen Augusta has an inventory of fine condition clothing and accessories from the eighteenth century through the 1930s. She has designer clothing, heirloom lace, and period costumes. Her inventory of accessories includes fans, shoes, corsets, bags and hats. Write for a mail order catalog.

Picture Window Antiques
61 Main Street
Poultney, VT 05764
(802) 287-2050
Specializing in men's, women's and children's clothing, Picture Window Antiques carries inventory from the Victorian age to the 1940s. They also rent costumes.

WASHINGTON

Madame & Co.
117 Yesler Way
Pioneer Square
Seattle, WA 98104
(206) 621-1728
With a wide selection of items, Madame & Co. carries ladies' fashions from many eras. Among their tempting offerings are lingerie, white petticoats, pantaloons, and wedding dress-
es—Edwardian, Victorian and deco—as well as other deco garments. They also carry antique laces, buttons, and trims dating as far back as the nineteenth century. They do fine restoration work as well.

Fritzi Ritz
3425 Freemont Place N.
Seattle, WA 98103
(206) 633-0929
With a speciality in fashions and accessories that date up to the 1950s, Fritzi Ritz has items for both men and women.

Isidore's Antique Clothing
1915 First Avenue
Seattle, WA 98101
(206) 441-7711
Isidore's carries high-end fashion for men and women from the turn of the century to the late 1940s. They also have an inventory of lace, fabrics, accessories and fancy clothing. One of several specialties is their selection of gabardine suits.

Rudy's Vintage Clothing and Antique
1424 First Avenue
Seattle, WA 98101
(206) 682-6586
With the largest selection of vintage wristwatches in the Northwest, Rudy's is a tough one to beat. In addition to timepieces, they carry men's and women's fashions, as well as vintage fabrics.

VINTAGE CLOTHING AND TEXTILE SHOWS

The shows listed below are known for their high quality and exclusive selection of dealers in vintage clothing and textiles. While general antique shows may include several vintage clothing and textiles dealers, most are entirely vintage clothing and fabric dealers.

Show promoters are listed by the location of their shows; therefore, some promoters appear under multiple state headings, since they promote shows in more than one location. Show dates vary from year to year, so call the promoter for the most current dates.

ARIZONA

High Noon
9929 Venice Boulevard
Los Angeles, CA 90034
(310) 202-9010

Wild West Collectors Show & Auction
Centennial Hall/
Sheraton Mesa Hotel
Mesa, AZ
Jan. Show

CALIFORNIA

Vintage Expositions
Box 391
Alamo, CA 94507
(415) 822-7227

Vintage Fashion Expo
Convention Center
Broadway & 10th
Oakland, CA
Jan. and Sept. Shows

Vintage Fashion Expo
Civic Auditorium
1855 Main (& Pico)
Santa Monica, CA
Oct., Dec. & Feb. Shows

Vintage Fashion Expo
The Concourse

8th & Brannan
San Francisco, CA
March Show

CONNECTICUT

The Maven Company, Inc. & The Young Management Company
P.O. Box 1538
Waterbury, CT 06721
(203) 758-3880

Semi-Annual Show and Sale of Vintage Clothing, Jewelry & Textiles
National Guard Armory
Armory Road & Rt. 108
Stratford, CT
Sept. & March Shows

Barrows Show Promotional, Ltd.
Box 141
Portland, CT 06480
(203) 342-2540

Greater Hartford Vintage Clothing & Jewelry Show & Sale
West Hartford, CT
Nov., Jan. & June Shows

ILLINOIS

Cat's Pajamas Productions
125 W. Main Street
West Dundee, IL 60118
(708) 428-8368

*Vintage Clothing &
Jewelry Show & Sale*
Hemmens Auditorium
Grove Avenue
at the Fox River
Elgin, IL
March & Oct. Shows

MASSACHUSETTS

The Textile Show Associates
384 Union Street
Portsmouth, NH 03801
(603) 430-8588

Sturbridge Textile Shows
Host Hotel, Route 20
Sturbridge, MA
May, July, Sept. & Dec.

Molly's Vintage Promotions
194 Amity Street
Amherst, MA 01002
(413) 549-6446

*Molly's Show and Sale of
Vintage Fashions &
Antique Textiles*
Holiday Inn
Holyoke, MA
Sept. Show

NEW JERSEY

Brimfield Associates
P.O. Box 1800
Ocean City, NJ 08226
(609) 926-1800

Atlantique City Show
Atlantic City
Convention Hall
Florida Avenue &
Boardwalk

Atlantic City, NJ
March and Oct. Shows

Stella Show Management Co.
163 Terrace Street
Haworth, NJ 07641
(201) 384-0010

*Garden State
International Antiques &
Jewelry Show*
Garden State Exhibit Ctr.
Somerset, NJ
Feb. & Aug. Shows

NEW YORK

Stella Show Mgmt. Co.
163 Terrace Street
Haworth, NJ 07641
(201) 384-0010

NY Coliseum Show
New York Coliseum
Columbus Circle
New York City, NY
Jan., Mar. & Oct. Shows

Manhattan Triple Pier Expo
Passenger Ship
Terminals 88, 90 & 92
New York City, NY
Feb. & Nov. Shows

Metropolitan Arts & Antiques Pavillion
110 West 19th Street
New York City, NY 10011
(212) 463-0200

Antique Textiles Shows
Metropolitan Arts &
Antiques Pavillion
110 W. 19th Street
New York, NY
Fall, Winter & Spring
Shows

Molly's Vintage Promotions
194 Amity Street
Amherst, MA 01002
(413) 549-6446

*Molly's Manhattan Show &
Sale of Vintage Fashion &
Antique Textiles*
200 Club at 200 Fifth Ave.
New York, NY
April Show

PENNSYLVANIA

Nadia
P.O. Box 156
Flourtown, PA 19301
(215) 643-1396

*Antique Vintage Clothing,
Textiles & Accessories
Show & Sale*
Adams Mark (Grand
Ballroom)
City Avenue &
Monument Road
Philadelphia, PA
Nov. & Feb. Shows

**Great Eastern
Productions**
R.D. #2, Box 141
Zionsville, PA 18092
(215) 967-2181

*Great Eastern U.S.
Jewelry, Vintage Fashions
& Textile Show & Sale*
Agricultural Hall,
Allentown Fairgrounds
17th & Chew Streets
Allentown, PA
May Show

Renningers Promotions
27 Bensinger Drive
Schuylkill Haven, PA
17972
(717) 385-0104

*Renningers Mid-Western
Classic*
Valley Forge
Convention Center
King of Prussia, PA
Feb. & March Shows

VIRGINIA

**David M. & Peter J.
Mancuso, Inc.**
Professional Show Mgmt.
P.O. Box 667
New Hope, PA 18938

*Williamsburg Vintage
Fashion and Jewelry Show*
Patrick Henry Inn
Route 60
Williamsburg, VA
Feb. Show

WASHINGTON

**Somewhere In Time
Promotions**
P.O. Box 88892
Seattle, WA 98138
(206) 531-4194

*Pacific Northwest Vintage
Fashion Market*
Seattle Ctr. Flag Pavillion
Seattle, WA
Sep. & March Shows

AUCTION HOUSES

Auction houses are currently taking a keen interest in vintage clothing. We predict this trend will continue through the century.

NEW YORK

William Doyle Galleries
175 East 87th Street
New York, NY 10128
(212) 427-2730
FAX: (212) 369-0892
For recorded announcement
of forthcoming auctions call:
(212) 427-4885

Christie's East
219 East 67th Street
New York, NY 10021
(212) 606-0400

CONSERVATORS, CONSERVATION STUDIOS, AND CONSERVATION SUPPLIERS

It is important to have professional people who are trained in conservation to restore antique pieces. Be sure to call first before sending them your pieces.

Marianna Klaiman
Textile Conservator/
Consultant
2 Sheridan Avenue
Waldwick, NJ 07463
(201) 652-5372 (by
appointment only)

Bryce Reveley
Gentle Arts
4500 Dryades Street
Studio B
New Orleans, LA 70115
(504) 895-5628

A. Newbold Richardson
Historic Preservation/
Costumes & Textiles
602 South View Terrace
Alexandria, VA 22314
(703) 684-0863 (by
appointment only)

Susan Becker Aziz
Conservator of Heirloom
Textiles
28-B Russell Street
Litchfield, CO 06759
(203) 567-1717
(by appointment only)

Judith Eisenberg
Textile Conservator
New York, NY
(212) 691-2638
(by appointment only)

If you need to find a conservator, a referral service is offered by the American Institute for the Conservation of Historic and Artistic Works. When contacting them, please be specific as to what your needs are and the exact piece you wish to have restored, so they can give you a conservator who specializes in your area of concern.

American Institute for the Conservation of Historic and Artistic Works
1717 K Street NW, Suite 301
Washington, D.C. 20006
(202) 452-9545

CONSERVATION STUDIOS

The Textile Conservation Workshop, Inc.
Main Street
South Salem, NY 10590
(215) 763-5805

Textile Conservation Laboratory
Cathedral of St. John the Divine
1047 Amsterdam Avenue
New York, NY 10025

CONSERVATION SUPPLIERS

Acid–free tissue and boxes can be ordered directly from suppliers.

Light Impressions
Rochester, NY
(800) 828-9859

University Products, Inc.
P.O. Box 101
Holyoke, MA 01041
(800) 628-1912

Talas
568 Broadway
Suite 107
New York, NY 10012
(212) 219-0770

MARKET TRENDS

The following prices are intended only as a guide to help familiarize you with vintage fashion. Keep in mind, there are always exceptions. The pricing of a vintage fashion is based on certain criteria. First is the condition of the item. Second is the quality or uniqueness of a piece. Third is the location where you are buying. Prices are going to be higher where there is greatest demand, very often where you'll find the better pieces.

The following list reflects current retail values which change according to the desirability of a piece. These are price ranges only and must be used to judge a garment with the criteria firmly in mind. They have been gathered by experts in hopes of making your collecting easier. **All values are for fine to mint condition wearable garments with good to excellent design features.**

Victorian petticoat . . . . $ 75–$300
Edwardian lingerie
    dresses *(c. 1900–1910)*. . . . . . . $200–$600
Victorian and Edwardian
    lace gowns . . . . $500–$2,000
1920s beaded dress
    (depending on fabric and bead work;
    extra for superior workmanship; if
    made in Paris, as high as $800) . . . . $125–$600

1920s embroidered silk shawl
  (depends on color and embroidery) . . . .$195–$500
1920s Egyptian silver shawl
  (depending on amount of silver) . . . . .$125–$550
1920s unusual cloche hat . . . .$125–$350
1920s enameled metal mesh purse . . .$125–$375
1920s silk stockings *(sheers,*
  pastels, clocks or embroidery) . . . .$ 30–$200
1920s/1930s silk velvet coat
  (depending on detail such as voided
  velvet, opera coat, distinctive collars,
  and beading, prices can be as high
  as $1,200) . . . .$300–$500
1920s/1930s man's tux vest . . . .$ 50–$100
1930s silk chiffon afternoon dress
  (condition is extremely important with
  chiffons; add extra for matching
  jacket ($450) . . . .$125–$275
1930s silk or satin nightgown
  (bias-cut) . . . .$ 65–$150
1930s satin wedding gown
  (bias-cut) (size is important) . . . .$275–$500
1930s silk chiffon dressing robe . . . . .$250–$300
1930s/1940s Borsolino man's hat . . . . .$150–$300
1930s/1940s man's linen Palm
  Beach suit . . . .$400–$550
1930s/1940s man's dinner jacket . . . . .$150–$200
1940s woman's basic gabardine
  suit jacket *(daytime)* . . . .$ 95–$350
1940s woman's evening beaded
  suit jacket *(depending on fabric,*
  condition, amount of decoration) . . . . .$450–$900
1940s man's painted silk tie
  (depends on subject) . . . .$ 20–$100
1940s man's photo tie
  (wider is better) . . . .$ 25–$ 75
1940s/1950s Hawaiian shirt *(depends*
  on size, interest and color) . . . .$ 20–$400
1940s/1950s Pendleton man's
  gabardine jacket . . . .$300–$450
1940s/1950s basic wool toppers . . . . .$ 35–$ 50

1940s/1950s toppers with
   passementerie ....$ 95–$550
1940s/1950s basic cocktail dress .....$ 50–$ 75
1940s/1950s silk cocktail dress
   (with unusual or exceptional design) ..$150–$300
1940s/1950s cotton or rayon
   day dresses *(depending on style
   and condition)* ....$ 35–$150
1950s woman's suit ....$ 95–$350
1950s capri pants ....$ 65–$125
1950s cashmere beaded sweater .....$ 50–$125
1950s cotton circle skirt
   *(add extra for the unusual or the
   extraordinary, up to $300)* ....$ 75–$125
1950s/1960s "prom dress" ....$ 50–$175
Embroidered silk Chinese jacket
   (depending on style and embroidery) ..$ 45–$225
Mexican handpainted skirt ....$100–$150

COUTURE PIECES: The following list reflects current auction prices. Auction selling prices are dependent upon the audience at any given time. It is important to preview an auction to check pieces closely for condition, uniqueness and desirability. These prices are only intended as a guide, to help familiarize you with market values of couture fashion.

Boue Soeurs,
   1920s lingerie dress ....$ 850–$1,500
Vionnet, 1920s little
   black dress ....$1,400–$2,500
Christian Dior,
   1960s ballgown ....$1,000–$3,000
Maggy Rouff,
   1940s dinner dress ....$ 250–$ 600

CHAPTER 5

INSTANT EXPERT QUIZ

1. In the last half of the nineteenth century, the fashion style was named for what Queen?

2. Aniline dyes in 1856 made what kind of change to ribbon and fabric?

3. In the late nineteenth century, what was a skirt made with straight panels called?

4. What fashion years are considered Edwardian?

5. What fashion term was used to describe the corseted silhouette of women in the early twentieth century?

6. What fine art influenced the dress designs and colors of courtier Paul Poiret in the teens?

7. What style of fashion did Gabrielle Chanel introduce in the twenties?

8. What Parisian accessories were popular in the twenties?

9. How did courtier Madeleine Vionnet's bias-cut affect dress design in the thirties?

10. Hollywood was the primary fashion inspiration for which decades?

11. Name three fabrics that were popular for thirties clothing.

12. Why did the fashions of the forties have regulation length jackets, without pockets or detail?

13. What constitutes the fashion called the "New Look" and why was it given that name?

14. What is the proper way to store vintage pieces?

15. Who was Jackie Kennedy's exclusive designer in the sixties?

16. When did sunglasses gain popularity?

17. Body painting, decals and paper fashions were all fads of which decade?

18. American designers came to the forefront in fashion during and after World War II, when Americans wanted fashions to complement their lifestyles. Name an American designer associated with this decade.

19. Hollywood's designers of the thirties, forties and fifties were very influential in setting fashion trends. Name a Hollywood designer.

20. When was it acceptable for brides to wear plaid?

Answers

1. *Queen Victoria*
2. *bright colors*
3. *a gored skirt*
4. *c. 1900 to 1910*
5. *S-shape or pigeon shape*
6. *Fauvism and/or Ballet Russes*
7. *uncluttered clothing and the little black dress*
8. *fabric flowers, small mesh purses, art deco compacts, feather fans, ribbons and trim, cloches*
9. *Dresses and gowns were slim and narrow over the hips, with a molded or draped effect.*
10. *1930s and 1940s*
11. *silk, satin, organdy, eyelet, piqué, gingham, corduroy, knits, wool, velvets, crepe, Lastex, rayons*
12. *World War II manufacturing restrictions*
13. *Christian Dior's 'New Look' is typified by soft shoulders, small waist and full midcalf skirt. It was the new look after WW II and was a change from the austerity of war-time clothing.*
14. *The best way to store them is with acid-free tissue and acid-free covered boxes in a temperature controlled environment.*
15. *Oleg Cassini*
16. *the 1950s*
17. *the 1960s*
18. *Claire McCardell, Carolyn Schnurer, Clare Potter, Hattie Carnegie, Nettie Rosenstein, Norman Norell, Adrian, Maurice Rentner*
19. *Adrian, Edith Head, Helen Rose*
20. *In the nineteenth century*

APPENDIX

GLOSSARY

à disposition: a special weave that produces a pattern; also the term used to describe a patterning method.

A-line: skirt or dress shaped like a capital A.

aigrette: a stiff tuft of egret or osprey tail feathers used as an ornament.

aniline dyes: dyes made from indigo, producing bright colors; invented in England in 1856.

appliqué: pieces of fabric sewn on a garment for decoration.

apron: a small piece of fabric worn over the front of clothing that ties in the back with self-fabric ties.

art deco: a bold, geometric style of decoration popular from 1925-1940.

art nouveau: a decorative style popular in the late 19th century and early 20th century which is distinguished by the use of flowing lines and flowers.

artificial silk: term given to rayon from 1890 to 1920.

bakelite: trade name for material made from heating phenol with formaldehyde; a popular pressed plastic for jewelry, buckles and buttons in the thirties.

ballgown: a full-skirted, ankle-length gown with décolleté neckline, usually made in rich fabrics.

ballet-length: mid-calf length

Ballets Russes: a series of ballets in Russia in the early 20th century. The oriental costumes with their rich fabrics and bright colors greatly influenced fashion.

bandanna: a large colored handkerchief, often figured.

battle jackets: (Eisenhower or bomber jacket) widely-cut jacket with long sleeves and pockets; buttons or zips up the front.

beret: a knitted or woven circular hat without a brim.

Bermuda shorts: shorts ending just above the knee.

bertha: a wide, deep lace collar, falling from an oval neckline and covering the shoulders of a dress.

bettina blouse: designed by Givenchy and named for his top Parisian model, Bettina Graziani. The blouse was made of shirting and had ruffled broderie anglaise sleeves and open neck.

bias cut: material cut diagonally across the grain allowing it to fall into a vertical drape that could be sculpted to the body; popular in films of the thirties; original designed by Madeleine Vionnet.

bikini: a very brief two-piece bathing suit.

bishop sleeve: popular style from the mid-19th century to the 1970s; a long dress sleeve that is full below the elbow and gathered at the wrist.

bloomers: full, loose trouser garments gathered at ankle or knee.

blouson top: a dress top that is pulled together at the waist causing it to puff out over the skirt.

boaters: popular hat for men in the late 19th century to 1940s and for women in the twenties; a hard, circular hat made of straw with a flat crown and ribbon band.

bobbi socks: short, white socks popular with teenagers in the fifties.

bodice: the upper part of a dress; in the 19th century, the bodice was boned and fitted; in the 20th century, bodice is used as a dressmaker's term for the top, front and back sections of a garment.

bodystocking: a leotard-shaped, fine knitted, pull-on garment worn under semi-transparent clothing; introduced in the sixties.

bolero: a short Spanish-style sleeveless bodice, worn open.

boning: stays sewn into garment for stiffening and to provide shape.

bonnet: a hat that covers the whole head and ties under the chin; popular in many styles in the 19th century.

bouclé: Fr. (to curl) a fabric that is knitted or woven from looped yarn, giving a nap to the fabric.

bouffant style: full or puffed-out style.

bowlers: a derby; a hard, round hat with crown and rolled brim; worn by men in the late 19th century up to WW II.

brocade: a rich, jacquard fabric with raised design, usually of figures or flowers; in silk, gold or silver threads.

broderie anglaise: also known as Swiss or Madeira embroidery; a white on white embroidery often used as trim.

bubble skirt: Pierre Cardin designed stiffened short-skirted bubble-shaped dresses in 1957.

burnous: a full cloak with a hood that is embellished with embroidery and tassels, originally of African origin.

busk: a knife-shaped piece of whalebone which was inserted in the front of a corset and held in place by the lacing.

bustle: a pad of stuffing worn under the skirt at or just below the waist to expand fullness to the back.

caftan: an ankle-length, silk or cotton garment with long wide sleeves and sash waist; used in various fashion designs.

calico: a sturdy, durable fabric of coarse cotton; usually dyed.

cape: a sleeveless outer garment fastened at the neck and worn like a cloak.

capri pants: popular pant style in the fifties; pants tapered to mid-calf.

cardigan: long-sleeved knitted sweater without a collar; made popular for women in the twenties by Gabrielle Chanel.

cartwheel hat: a hat with a shallow crown and exaggerated, straight brim, usually in straw.

catsuit: a zip or button front garment that is all in one piece.

Celenese rayon: Celenese is the trademark name for the manufacturer of rayon.

Chantilly lace: a bobbin lace often in black with a floral and dots motif on a fine background; design outlined by a heavier thread (cordonnet).

chaps: leg-coverings worn by cowboys for protection.

chatelaine: popular in the 19th century to carry practical items by the woman of the household; made of steel and hung down from waistband.

chemise: a shirt-like garment worn as an undergarment by women.

chemise dress: a no-waisted straight-lined dress made popular in the twenties by Gabrielle Chanel.

chenille: fabric made with cotton, silk, rayon or wool that has a fur-like texture.

Chesterfield coat: After WW II, a long black velvet collared coat worn by young women. In the nineteenth century, a man's grey wool coat with fitted waist.

cheviot: woolen fabric used for coats and suits.

chiffon: a light, gauzy fabric made from finely twisted threads of silk, wool or synthetics; popular for scarves or evening wear.

cinch belt: a wide elastic belt popular with skirts of the fifties.

circle skirt: round skirt cut from one or two pieces of fabric; popular in the fifties.

cloak: a full-cut outer garment without sleeves that covers the body.

cloche: Fr. (bell): a tight-fitting hat covering the head, with or without a brim and worn low over the brow; popular from 1915 to 1935.

cloisonné: enameling done with thin metal bands dividing the colors.

clutch purse: handbag without straps; popular in a variety of shapes and sizes.

confections: nineteenth-century women's outer garments such as cloaks, mantels and capes.

coolie hat: a slanted one-piece hat often made of straw.

corduroy: a durable cut-pile cotton or rayon with vertical ribbing of wide or narrow cords.

corset: worn under a dress in the nineteenth century to achieve a smaller waist. It was made of stays inserted in the fabric and then laced tightly.

Cossack styled: fashions influenced by Russian dress, characterized by full, flowing skirts tied with sashes, full pants tucked in boots and tall fur hats.

cotton: a fabric produced from the fibers of the cotton plant, used especially for summer garments and underwear.

coul: a drape attached to the neck of a garment that can be used as a hood or neckline drape.

couture: (abbrev. for haute couture) term used for custom-made or high fashion clothing as opposed to clothes that are mass-produced.

cravat: man's necktie

crepe: a light, soft fabric with a crinkled texture made from natural and synthetic materials.

crepe de Chine: crepe made from raw silk.

crepe georgette: sheer creped fabric made from silk, silk and cotton, silk and rayon and other mixtures; often used for evening wear and blouses.

crinoline cage: made popular by Empress Eugenie in the 1850s, which allowed skirts to stay very full and round.

crochet: needlework made by looping yarn or thread with a hooked needle.

cubism: an abstract art movement developed in Paris in the early twentieth century that influenced textile designers to use bold, flat, geometric shapes and patterns.

cuirass: a jacket bodice that is fitted to the hipline.

culotte: divided skirt into two legs but giving the effect of a full skirt.

cummerbund: a wide waist cloth worn by both men and women in the twentieth century; a substitute for the man's previously worn waistcoat.

cutaway: a man's formal coat with tails, where front of coat is cut away from the waist to the back.

dacron: trade name of DuPont manufacturing; polyester fabric from early fifties.

damask: a luxurious decorative woven silk fabric with pattern as part of weave; self-colored. In the 19th century, used for women's clothing. In the 20th century, usually used in home furnishings.

dart: a pointed tuck sewn inside of a garment to shape the garment to the body.

décolletage: (décolleté neckline) low-cut neckline of blouse or dress, exposing neck and back or shoulders.

denim: a sturdy cotton twill fabric made from white and blue threads.

déshabillés: very fancy tea gowns popular in the late nineteenth centuries and early twentieth centuries.

dirndl: a skirt that is full and loosely pleated at the waist.

djellabah: a long, hooded Moroccan cloak with full wide sleeves, worn with an open neck; popular in sixties and seventies.

dolman sleeve: made as an extension of the bodice, not set into the armhole; full wide sleeve at the armhole and narrow at the wrist; very popular in the thirties; also called batwing.

double breasted: jacket with two rows of buttons for front closure.

drawers: knickers made of cotton or linen and worn as underwear.

Edwardian: an elaborate style of dress associated with clothing styles during the reign of King Edward VII (1901-1910).

Eisenhower jacket: a jacket introduced in WW II and made popular by General Eisenhower. Also called battle or bomber jacket.

Elizabethan collar: decorative, high-necked collar.

embroidery: decorative needlework done on fabric by hand or machine.

Empire waist: a low-cut dress gathered under the bustline.

Empress Eugenie hat: small hat designed by Adrian and worn tilted forward to one side. Named for the Empress Eugenie of France.

ensemble: a coordinated outfit.

envelope bag: rectangular purse without a strap and with an envelope-style closure.

epaulette: shoulder strap on coat or jacket used for decoration.

Eton suit: suit worn by boys in the late nineteenth centuries and early twentieth centuries; characterized by a short, square jacket.

eyelet: lightweight fabric with small threadbound holes making up the design.

faille: a soft, middleweight, slightly ribbed fabric with a slight luster that is woven in silk, cotton or rayon.

Fair Isle sweater: sweater with knitted band across the shoulders, neck and chest in a multi-colored geometric pattern.

Fauvism: art movement of the early 1900s that influenced fashion and fabric design with the use of flat, two-dimensional shapes in bright colors.

fedora: a soft felt hat with brim and tapered crown with center crease; popular men's style at the end of the nineteenth century to the fifties.

felt: a fabric made by bonding fibers of cotton, fur or wool; used primarily in making hats.

Femina: fashion review from 1901-1956.

fez: cylinder-shaped hat with tassel on top.

fishnet: large open-weave knitted net.

fishtail train: train shaped like the tail of a fish.

flannel: a household term for woolen fabrics.

foulard: printed design on soft silk used to make neckties and scarves.

frock coat: 19th century men's formal attire; knee-length coat with tails, collar, and back vents; used for design of women's coats in the 20th century.

gabardine: a strong, tightly-woven fabric with fine ribbed effect made of cotton, wool or rayon twill.

georgette: silk or rayon fabric; popular for evening wear.

gigot sleeve: leg-of-mutton sleeve.

gimp: flat cord of silk or wool used in decoration of clothing.

gingham: a medium weight cotton/linen fabric woven into checks with predyed yarns.

godet: a fabric of triangular shape that is inserted into a garment to give it fullness.

gored skirts: skirts made from tapered strips of fabric that widen toward the hemline.

granny gown: old-fashioned clothing style with long, full skirts; popular in late sixties to early seventies.

grommet: metal-made eyelet in a garment.

grosgrain: heavily ribbed, closely woven silk fabric used in millinary.

hacking jackets: a fitted, single-breasted jacket that flares from the waist with a single back-vent; originally used as a riding jacket.

halo hat: hat worn at the back of the head with the brim acting as a frame for the face.

halter: a neckline style that is high in front, ties at back of neck and reveals back and shoulders.

harem pants: a full, ankle-length divided skirt or pants based on Turkish women's trousers.

Harris tweed: originally referred to a handloomed wool.

Hawaiian shirt: colorful shirts depicting fruit, flowers and island themes.

helmet: a hat that covers and fits close to the head.

hobble skirt: a skirt style introduced by Paul Poiret that was narrow and tight-fitting from knee to ankle, making walking difficult; popular between 1910-1914.

homburgs: a man's stiff, felt hat with thin rolled brim and center crease crown; popularized by Edward VII, Prince of Wales, when visiting Homburg, Germany.

horseshoe collar: a collar with a deep U-shape.

hot pants: c. 1970s term used for short pants.

Ivy League: American dress style worn by college students on the East coast; characterized for men by gray flannel suits and button-down shirts with narrow-striped tie; for women, kilt, blazer, sweater and string of pearls.

jacquard: decorative weave created on a jacquard loom, especially for brocades and damasks. These fabrics have woven-in patterns.

jams: men's bright-colored bathing suits styled as shorts with drawstring waist. Popular in the sixties.

jersey: a soft, stretchy, knitted fabric popular in the twenties.

jumper: a sleeveless dress with a round or square neckline, worn over a blouse.

jumpsuit: a zip-front, all-in-one piece suit with long sleeves and legs.

Kate Greenaway: (1846-1903) English book illustrator who influenced children's dress styles in the nineteenth century, with empire-line dresses, bonnets, smocks and ruffles.

kilt: tartan cloth skirt which is pleated and made to overlap in the front where it is secured by buckles and a large pin.

kimono: (Japanese) loose-fitting robe with wide sleeves and worn with a wide waist sash.

knickerbockers: knickers

knickers: full-cut pants gathered at knees.

lamé: usually a gold or silver fabric woven with metallic threads; popular in the thirties for evening wear.

lapel: part of jacket's neckline that can turn back or fold over.

Lastex: U.S. Rubber Co. trade name for elastic yarn fabrics.

lawn: a fine, plain woven, sheer cotton or linen fabric with crisp finish.

leg-of-mutton sleeve: a sleeve that is tight-fitting from the wrist to the elbow and very full from elbow to shoulder where it is gathered to fit into the armhole; used in late nineteenth century on blouse or bodice.

leotard: a one-piece long-sleeved spandex suit.

linen: a strong, natural fabric woven from fibers of the flax plant that can be made in fine or coarse textures.

lucite: transparent plastic.

Lurex: Dow Badische Co. trade name for metallic fiber yarn knitted with cotton, nylon, rayon, silk or wool; made in 1940s.

Madras plaid: Indian cotton plaid.

maillot: one-piece bathing suit that is tight fitting.

malacca: type of wood used to make canes and parasol handles in the 19th century.

mandarin jacket: a Chinese-styled jacket with small stand-up collar fastened in front or on the shoulder.

mantle: woman's outer garment of the late nineteenth century in the form of a waist or hip-length cloak with hood.

maxi: ankle or floor-length skirt; popular in the sixties.

micro: very short skirt; popular in the sixties.

midi: mid-calf length skirt; popular in the late sixties.

mini: above-the-knee length skirt; popular from 1962-1970.

mohair: loosely woven fabric made from angora wool.

moiré silk: late nineteenth century silk fabric with water effect.

monastic dress: Claire McCardell design of 1938; very full and flared from the shoulders with optional belt.

Mondrian, Piet: (1872-1944) artist who painted in cubist style and influenced fashion designer, Yves Saint Laurent in the 60s with his grid-like divisions of flat colors.

motif: a recurring figure in the pattern of a design.

mousseline: a fine plain woven fabric in cotton, silk or wool having a stiff finish; popular in the nineteenth century.

muff: used to keep hands warm and made in a variety of pillow-like shapes; popular accessory in the late nineteenth century.

muslin: plain, cotton, woven fabric made in a variety of weights.

Nehru suit: jacket with stand-up collar and button front that was popular in white in the sixties.

Norfolk jacket: a wool tweed, hip-length jacket with large patch pockets, front and back box pleats and self-material belt; worn by men in the nineteenth century and, in 1890, worn by women for sporting events.

nylon: household term for fabric made from synthetics; popular for stockings and pantyhose.

op-art: art style of the sixties that influenced fashion and fabrics with optical circles, squares and spirals.

organdy: a sheer, light cotton fabric that is stiffened by chemicals. After WW II, organdy was made of rayon or silk.

pageboys: Fifties' curled under hairstyle.

pagoda sleeve: a three-quarter length sleeve, wider at the elbow and often with tiers of flounces and lace undersleeve.

panniers: a framework used to expand the upper sides of a skirt.

pareo: brightly covered wrapped skirts.

parure jewelry: a set of jewels that match and worn together; in the nineteenth century, consisted of earrings, necklace, bracelet, brooch, rings and head ornament.

passementerie: decorative trim for an article of clothing; braiding, beads, gimp, cording in various combinations.

patent leather: high-gloss material used on shoes and purses since the thirties.

pavé: in jewelry, setting stones very close together.

peacoat: a heavy, double-breasted, hip-length jacket originally worn by sailors.

pencil skirt: a slim skirt cut in one line from hips to hem.

peplum: a short skirt attached to the bodice or jacket that flares out over the hip.

petticoat: nineteenth-century women's underskirt of fine fabrics.

picture hat: a wide brimmed hat with high crown and usually decorated with ribbons and flowers.

pillbox hat: small, brimless hat with straight sides and flat top.

piping: a thin tube-like strip of fabric cut on the bias and used as an edging on a garment.

piqué: woven cotton, silk, or spun rayon fabric with length-wise cording.

platform sole: a thick sole on a shoe; popular in the forties and seventies.

plique-a-jour: enameling that looks like stained glass.

point de gaze: needlepoint lace of floral motif done on net ground.

poke bonnet: a bonnet with a forward deep brim that ties under the chin.

poncho: a square fabric with center opening for head.

pongee: an écru colored fabric with cross-wise ribbing, originally made from silk but popular in twentieth century cotton blends.

poplin: a sturdy, ribbed, plain-woven fabric made from combinations of silk, rayon, wool or cotton.

popover dress: Claire McCardell dress design of 1942; wrap-front and large pockets designed to be worn in the home.

prairie look: Ralph Lauren design in the seventies; white petticoat under denim skirt.

Princess line: slim-fitting dress line made without a waist seam; waist was created by vertical panels of fabric.

psychedelic: popular design of the sixties; irregular shapes and bright colors.

Quiana: wrinkle-free nylon introduced by Dupont in the 1960s.

rayon: synthetic fabric made by cellulose solution; often referred to as artificial silk.

rayon crepe: creped rayon.

ready-mades: term used in the nineteenth century for partly-made clothing that could be bought at a department store and then completed to one's own specifications. Mourning clothes were the first ready-mades.

ready-to-wear: term used to describe pre-made clothing that can be bought and worn "off the rack." Also used to describe the ready-to-wear industry.

reticules: nineteenth century small purse; made of soft fabrics with cord tie and worn held from the wrist.

rhinestone: glass or imitation stones used for decoration.

robe de style: a full-skirted, calf-length dress with a close-fitting bodice and natural or low waistline.

sack dress: a loosely shaped dress which tapers at the knees.

sailor suit: children's dress style at the turn of the century based on navy uniform.

sari: an Indian woman's outer garment made by one length of fabric of colored silk or cotton, wrapped at waist to make the skirt, with remaining part worn over the shoulder.

sarong: a length of fabric wrapped around the body and tied at the waist.

Sassoon, Vidal: (1929-) English hairstylist popular in the sixties and seventies for his layered and sculptured cuts that were compatible with the fashions.

sateen: usually a cotton weave made with satin that is strong and glossy.

satin: a smooth, lustrous fabric made from finely woven silk or rayon threads; the underside is dull.

sequin: a small disc of shiny metal or plastic that is used for trim.

serge: worsted fabric of twill weave originally made in silk or wool.

shawl: a square or rectangular piece of fabric worn wrapped around the shoulders.

sheath: a straight, figure-fitting dress.

shepherdess-style: a high-waisted dress with a bell-shaped skirt.

shift: simple, unconstructed dress in 20th century fashion.

shirring: two or more rows of gathering used as decoration on a garment.

shirtwaist: women's blouses in late nineteenth centuries/early twentieth century.

shirtwaist dress: a tailored, knee-length dress with long sleeves, a collar and usually a belt; first popular in the forties.

shrug jacket: abbreviated jacket.

silk: a fine fabric having a sheen and made of natural fibers produced by silkworms.

single breasted: row of single buttons for closure on a jacket.

slash pockets: side pockets

smocked dress: decorative stitching on the yoke of a child's dress.

snood: a knotted or woven net used to cover hair at the back of the head; sometimes attached to hats.

spaghetti ties: thin fabric strings that tie on the shoulders.

Spencer jacket: a nineteenth century woman's short, waist-length jacket worn as an outer garment or indoors over evening dress.

sportswear: American term for everyday or casual wear.

Stetson: American manufacturer's trade name.

stiletto heel: shoe with high, narrow heel; originated in Italy.

stole: a long, rectangualr wrap worn around the shoulders.

surrealism: a twentieth century art and literature movement characterized by fantasy or dream-like qualities. Elsa Schiaperelli's fashions often had surrealistic themes.

sweater set: matching pullover and cardigan sweaters, worn together.

sweetheart neckline: heart-shaped neckline, first popular in the forties.

table-top neckline: a sculptured neckline.

tafetta: a finely woven silk or faux silk fabric that is stiff and glossy.

tatting: handmade knotted lace made with cotton or linen thread.

tea gowns: mid-nineteenth century at-home gown designed to wear with loosened corset; by 1870s, gowns became very elaborate in fancy fabrics, lace, and ruffles.

tiaras: small crowns

tooled work: designs carved into leather.

topper: full, hip-length coat with shawl collar and turned-up cuffs; popular in the forties and fifties.

topstitching: decorative row of hand or machine-made stitching.

toque: various styles of head-hugging caps without a brim.

toreador pants: tight pants laced at the knee.

tournure: (bustle) French term popular in the late nineteenth century.

train: long, rectangular piece of fabric attached to back of dress at waist or shoulders.

trapeze dress: Yves Saint Laurent designed this dress in 1958; a tent shape dress that was cut wide and full, knee-length, and fell free from shoulders in the back.

trenchcoats: a military style raincoat of lightweight wool or cotton blend.

trompe l'oeil: optical illusion created by knitting a design into the garment.

tucks: a series of folds sewn and pressed down on fabric; used as decoration on a dress.

tulle: a fine, machine-made net fabric of silk, gauze or nylon.

tunic: a straight, sleeveless, loose-fitting garment with many fashion manifestations.

turban: originally a long scarf wrapped around the head; used by milliners to construct a hat style, especially popular in the thirties and forties.

tweed: a textured fabric woven of different colored wools.

twill: durable weave used often for cottons and wools. A twill pattern is usually recognizable by its diagonal wales.

Valenciennes lace: a light bobbin lace named for a lace making town on French/Belgium border; characterized by small holes surrounding the toiles (design); no cordonnet (raised outlining thread) and is usually made in a floral motif.

vareuse dress: Dior design in fifties based on the French fisherman smock; loose hip-length garment with stand-away collar.

veil: thin piece of fabric that covers the face; made in a variety of fabrics and lengths.

velour: velvet-like fabric made from natural or synthetic fibers.

velvet: a soft fabric made from a warp pile weave; the warp forms a smooth, dense pile of loops which may be pressed one way (panne) or stand erect; made from silk, cotton or synthetics; the underside is plain.

vinyl: plastic

waistcoats: man's sleeveless garment worn under jacket and over a shirt; often embroidered and made of silk.

warp prints: a patterning method whereby dyes are printed on a warp before weaving into cloth; the warp threads shift in the process and produce a somewhat blurred pattern.

wasp waist: tiny waist

wet-look: cire fabrics made by the combination of wax, heat and pressure on fabric to produce wet-like effect.

wool: strong fibers obtained from sheep.

worsted wool: a woolen fabric made from smooth yarn that is particularly durable.

wrap-around dress: twentieth century dress style that overlaps at the waist.

yoke: the upper part of a piece of clothing that fits across the bust, across the back behind the shoulders and holds up the rest of the garment.

BIBLIOGRAPHY

Amphlett, Hilda. *Hats: A History of Fashion in Headwear*. Buckinghamshire, G.B.: Richard Sadler Ltd., 1974.

Armstrong, Nancy. *The Book of Fans*. New York: Mayflower Books, Inc., 1978.

Beard, Tyler. *100 Years of Western Wear*. Salt Lake City: Gibbs-Smith Publishers, 1993.

Bell, Quentin. *On Human Finery*. New York: Schocken Books, 1976.

Braun-Ronsdorf, M. *The History of the Handkerchief*. Leigh-on-Sea, England: F. Lewis Publishers, Ltd., 1967.

Callister, J. Herbert. *Dress from Three Centuries*: Hartford, Conn.: Wadsworth Atheneum, 1976.

Carter, Ernestine. *The Changing World of Fashion: 1900 to the Present*. New York: G. P. Putnam and Sons, 1977.

Clark, Fiona. *Hats*. London: The Anchor Press Ltd., 1982.

Coleman, Elizabeth Ann. *The Opulent Era: Fashions of Worth, Doucet and Pingat*. Brooklyn: Thames and Hudson for the Brooklyn Museum, 1989.

Crawford, T. S. *A History of the Umbrella*. New York: Taplinger Publishing Company, 1970.

Cumming, Valerie. *Exploring Costume History, 1500-1900*. Great Britain: Anchor Press, Ltd., 1981.

D'Assailly, Gisele. *Ages of Elegance: Five Thousand Years of Fashion and Frivolity*. Greenwich, Conn: New York Graphic Society, Ltd., 1968

de Vere Green, Bertha. *Fans Over the Ages*. New York: A. S. Barnes & Company, Inc., 1979.

Engelmeier, Regine and Peter W. Engelmeier, eds. *Fashion in Film*. Munich: Prestel-Verlag, 1990.

Epstein, Diana and Millicent Safro. *Buttons*. New York: Harry N. Abrams, Inc., 1991.

Ettinger, Roseann. *Handbags*. Westchester, PA: Schiffer Publishing Ltd., 1991.

Ewing, Elizabeth. *Dress and Undress: A History of Women's Underwear*. Great Britain: Drama Book Specialists, 1978.

_____. *History of Children's Costume*. New York: Charles Scribner and Sons, 1977.

_____. *History of 20th Century Fashion*. New York: Charles Scribner and Sons, 1974.

Gibbings, Sarah. *The Tie*. New York: Barron's, 1990.

Ginsburg, Madeleine. *Paris Fashions: The Art Deco Style of the 1920s*. New York: W. H. Smith Publishers, Inc., 1989.

Glynn, Prudence with Madeleine Ginsburg. *In Fashion: Dress in the Twentieth Century*. New York: Oxford University Press, 1978.

Howell, Georgina. *In Vogue: 75 Years of Style*. London: Conde Naste Books, 1991.

Hunt, Marsha. *The Way We Wore: Styles of the 1930s and 40s*. Fallbrook, CA: Fallbrook Publishing Ltd., 1993.

Kennett, Frances. *The Collectors' Book of Fashion*. New York: Crown Publishers, Inc., 1983.

_____. *Secrets of the Couturiers*. New York: Simon & Schuster, 1984.

Ketchum, William C. Jr. *Western Memoribilia*. Maplewood, NJ: Rutledge Books, Inc., 1980.

Kneitel, Ken, Bill Maloney, and Andrea Quinn. *The Great American T-Shirt*. New York: The New American Library, Inc., 1976.

Lee, Sarah Tomerlin. *American Fashion*. New York: The Fashion Institute of Technology, 1975.

Leneck, Lena and Gideon Bosker. *Making Waves*. San Francisco: Chronicle Books, 1989.

Lurie, Alison. *The Language of Clothes*. New York: Random House, 1981.

Lynam, Ruth, ed. *Couture: An Illustrated History of the Great Paris Designers and their Creations*. Garden City, N.: Doubleday and Company, Inc., 1972.

Mayor, Susan. *A Collector's Guide to Fans*. Secaucus, NJ: Wellfleet Books, 1990.

McConathy, Dale. *Hollywood Costume: Glamour, Glitter, Romance*. New York: Harry N. Abrams, 1976.

Meller, Susan and Joost Elffers. *Textile Designs*. New York: Harry N. Abrams, 1991.

Milbank, Caroline Rennolds. *New York Fashion: The Evolution of American Style*. New York: Harry N. Abrams, Inc., 1989.

_____. *Couture: The Great Designers*. New York: Stewart, Tabori and Chang, Inc., 1985.

Mulvagh, Jane. *Vogue: History of Twentieth Century Fashion*. New York: Viking, 1988.

Murphy, Brian. *The World of Weddings: An Illustrated Celebration*. New York: Grosset & Dunlap, 1978.

Reedstrom, Ernest Lisle. *Historic Dress of the Old West*. New York: Blandford Press, 1986.

Robinson, Julian. *Fashion in the 30s*. London: Oresko Books, Ltd., 1978.

_____. *The Golden Age of Style: Art Deco Fashion Illustration*. New York: Harcourt Brace Jovanovich, 1976.

Schroeder, Joseph J. Jr. *The Wonderful World of Ladies' Fashion*. Chicago: Follett Publishing Company, 1971.

Severn, Bill. *Hand in Glove*. New York: David McKay Company, Inc., 1965.

Shields, Jody. *Hats*. New York: Clarkson Potter, 1991.

Sichel, Marion. *History of Children's Costume*. London: Batsford Academic and Educationial, Ltd., 1983.

Stein, Kurt. *Canes & Walking Sticks*. York, PA: G. Shumway, 1974.

Taylor, Lou. *Mourning Dress: A Costume and Social History*. London: George Allen and Unwin, 1983.

Thieme, Otto Charles. Elizabeth Ann Coleman, Michelle Oberly, Patricia Cunningham. *With Grace & Favour*. Cincinnati: Cincinnati Art Museum, 1993.

Tober, Barbara. *The Bride: A Celebration*. New York: Harry N. Abrams, Inc., 1984.

Wilcox, R. Turner. *The Mode in Costume*. New York: Charles Scribner and Sons, 1958.

Yarwood, Doreen. *European Costume: 4,000 Years of Fashion*. New York: Bonanza Books, 1975.

INDEX